"The phrases 'public intellectuals' and 'common good' are often misunderstood and misappropriated. But confusion over their meanings does not diminish their importance—inside and outside of Christian discourse. This impressive volume assembles leading experts and practitioners whose work and lives shed light on what it means for Christians to engage in public discourse, and the social ends toward which that engagement points."

John D. Inazu, Sally D. Danforth Distinguished Professor of Law and Religion and professor of political science, Washington University in St. Louis

"We are alive at a time of profound disorientation. We know instinctively the pace of change is accelerating and that we can't comprehend the scope of overlapping crises everywhere we turn. It's a moment that cries out for public intellectuals— truth tellers who help light our way forward. Yet as our society fragments and diversifies, it is increasingly difficult for us to agree on what truth even is. Because I am a journalist, I grapple constantly with this call to truth telling. How do we get to truth, and how do we inform the world? After reading *Public Intellectuals and the Common Good*, I am now reconsidering and expanding how I view this role. It may not be enough for us simply to tell truthful stories—we also have an active role to play as moral contributors to the common good."

Deborah Caldwell, chief executive officer and publisher, Religion News Service

"We're in great need of a Christian public voice amid the ravages of Trumpism. In this collection of compelling, invigorating essays, there is encouragement and modeling for how Christians can speak up in service to the common good. I read these essays amid the double pandemic of COVID-19 and white supremacist backlash. Here's a book needed now more than ever."

William H. Willimon, professor of the practice of Christian ministry at Duke University Divinity School

"At a time when separate identities and discord are champi⸗   ⸗rward, this collection of essays offers hope in seeking the 'com⸗   ⸗hen the microphone has been co-opted by those who   ⸗e- claim the microphone by bringing us together   ⸗ower has become a target, this collection calls f⸗   ⸗e essays invite those within the evangelical mo⸗⸗   ⸗n and those outside the evangelical movement to ⸗   ⸗naries than the stereotypes portray. It deserves a wide rea⸗

Gregory E. Sterling, dean and Lillian Claus Profess⸗   ⸗estament at Yale

"While some fear that the role of the public intellectual has been overpowered by social media platforms on which anyone can claim to be an authority or influencer, *Public Intellectuals and the Common Good* makes the case for pursuing and honoring the vocation of the public intellectual. Whether as theologians, scholars, journalists, or social activists, Christians have been called to identify and argue for a vision of human flourishing that crosses religious and cultural boundaries, making complex ideas accessible for all citizens. These provocative essays explore both the theoretical views and personal practices of Christian public intellectuals in the United States, who serve as prophetic voices in an age of incivility."

Susan VanZanten, assistant vice president of mission and spiritual life
and dean of Christ College, Valparaiso University

"'Public intellectual' and 'common good' are two terms that have lost much of their valence in our frayed and polarized culture. While acknowledging the gap, the essays in this volume call for a renewal of these ideals and present concrete ways to reengage for the good of us all. A book of wisdom worth serious attention."

Timothy George, research professor of divinity at Beeson Divinity School,
Samford University

"Can there be an authentic Christian voice in the public square? Can the church contribute to the common good in the context of polarization, fragmentation, and anti-intellectualism? This timely volume of perceptive essays offers insight into some of the most important issues of our day. It deserves careful consideration and widespread discussion."

Jeffrey P. Greenman, president and professor of theology and ethics at Regent College

Public Intellectuals and the Common Good

Christian Thinking for Human Flourishing

Edited by Todd C. Ream, Jerry Pattengale,

and Christopher J. Devers

Foreword by George M. Marsden

ivp

Academic

An imprint of InterVarsity Press
Downers Grove, Illinois

InterVarsity Press
P.O. Box 1400, Downers Grove, IL 60515-1426
ivpress.com
email@ivpress.com

InterVarsity Press® is the book-publishing division of InterVarsity Christian Fellowship/USA®, a movement of students and faculty active on campus at hundreds of universities, colleges, and schools of nursing in the United States of America, and a member movement of the International Fellowship of Evangelical Students. For information about local and regional activities, visit intervarsity.org.

Scripture quotations, unless otherwise noted, are from the New Revised Standard Version of the Bible, copyright 1989 by the Division of Christian Education of the National Council of the Churches of Christ in the USA. Used by permission. All rights reserved.

While any stories in this book are true, some names and identifying information may have been changed to protect the privacy of individuals.

Cover design and image composite: David Fassett
Interior design: Jeanna Wiggins
Image: tablet and newspaper: © John Lamb / DigitalVision / Getty Images

ISBN 978-0-8308-5481-3 (print)
ISBN 978-0-8308-5482-0 (digital)

Printed in the United States of America ∞

InterVarsity Press is committed to ecological stewardship and to the conservation of natural resources in all our operations. This book was printed using sustainably sourced paper.

Library of Congress Cataloging-in-Publication Data
A catalog record for this book is available from the Library of Congress.

P	25	24	23	22	21	20	19	18	17	16	15	14	13	12	11	10	9	8	7	6	5	4	3	2	1
Y	38	37	36	35	34	33	32	31	30	29	28	27	26	25	24	23	22	21

Contents

Foreword

George M. Marsden

Public Intellectuals and the Common Good is a most helpful guide for thinking about the role of Christian public intellectuals in America today. The editors adopt a broad approach as to what constitutes a public intellectual, and they wisely focus on the common good as the proper goal of Christian intellectual life.

In recent years Christians have sometimes suggested that there is a decline in the number of Christian public intellectuals, asking, "Where is our Reinhold Niebuhr?" That is an understandable question, but I think it is also misleading. There are certainly more explicitly Christian public intellectuals today in America than there were a generation ago. That is especially so among the sorts of Christians whom this book is directed toward, who might be classed as those who subscribe to something like what C. S. Lewis called mere Christianity. These include Protestants and Catholics, and especially the variety of Protestants who might be classed as traditionalist or broadly evangelical in the theological sense of that term. During the past thirty years or so there has been a remarkable renaissance among such Christian intellectuals, especially of the more or less evangelical sort. One index is simply the large number of excellent books by such authors being published not only by strong Christian presses but also by mainstream university and trade presses. Though some of these books are technical or strictly in the theological disciplines, addressed only to audiences of like-minded Christians, many others express broader cultural concern and are addressed not only to Christians but to diverse audiences. Many of these publications, furthermore, include reflections on the common good that are informed by Christian concerns. These days, in addition, such intellectuals do not have to rely just on books or opportunities to offer op-eds or to contribute articles to major magazines. They can immediately address potentially wide audiences through all sorts of electronic media.

While many of the authors in this volume think of the category of public intellectuals as including any intellectual whose work reaches diverse public audiences, others would limit the term to only those intellectuals whose work has a *large* impact on their culture. That latter definition then leads to the Reinhold Niebuhr question. It seems to me, though, that drawing the line quantitatively is unduly restrictive. This volume offers many examples of Christian public intellectuals who reach substantial audiences that are nonetheless relatively small in comparison to a Niebuhr or a Martin Luther King Jr. The reason why today there is no one who seems as relatively prominent as Niebuhr or King is that our culture is far more diversified and fragmented than it was in the mid-twentieth century. Not that there were not plenty of vituperative divisions in that era of so-called consensus. Lots of people thought that Niebuhr and especially King were of the devil. Still, such prominent thinkers, or, let's say, a William F. Buckley Jr., could reach large audiences on at least one side of the cultural divide. And in the mid-twentieth century there were still good grounds for hope that appeals to common principles of enlightened reason or to shared ideals from Western civilization and the Judeo-Christian heritage could resonate broadly.

Today, as many people have pointed out, the fragmentation is more severe. That is seen in the dysfunction of our public media. In the mid-twentieth century we had three major TV news networks that all similarly attempted to address the whole public. We had identifiably leading newspapers and magazines. If someone appeared on the cover of *Time*, it was a matter of wide public significance. Today the news is mostly tailored to politically oriented subgroups. With electronic media, anyone can present oneself as a public intellectual or as an authority on controversial issues. Controversial partisan political issues draw more attention than any others. So Christian intellectuals, like everyone else, are tempted to become preoccupied with divisive political controversies.

That brings us to the matter of addressing the common good. Everyone, of course, thinks that their view of the culture or of the next political necessity is in the interest of the common good—and sometimes that is indeed the case. But as Jonathan Haidt and Greg Lukianoff have helpfully observed, the current state of our culture seems especially suited to bring out the human instinct for tribalism. That tendency toward tribalistic thinking is accentuated by our culture's laudable emphasis in recent generations on diversity. Identity politics encourages the tendency to divide the world between "them" and "us" and to interpret the views of those who differ from us in the least generous ways possible.[1]

As the present volume emphasizes, Christians ought to be among those who are working the hardest to find common ground. While Christians speak from distinct points of view that lots of people do not share, Christians are remarkably diverse in ethnicity, nationality, social class, outlooks on social and political issues, and in most other ways. So Christians of all people should not first be looking how to promote their own social subgroup or to promote only the welfare

---

[1]Jonathan Haidt and Greg Lukianoff, in *The Coddling of the American Mind* (New York: Penguin, 2019), especially 33-57.

of other Christians, but should first be seeking how to address the common good.

For keeping that priority in the foreground it is particularly helpful to be reminded that in the current age Christians are not called to rule "all the kingdoms of the world" (as Satan puts it to Jesus in Matthew 4:8), but rather to be salt and light (Matthew 5:13-16) in a fallen world filled with evil, strife, and turmoil. For that we must be among those who reflect the sacrificial light of the crucified Christ. To be effective Christian communicators we need first to be persons and parts of communities whose manner and deeds manifest love for those who differ from us. People are much more often convinced by what people do and by a generous demeanor than they are by mere arguments. The body of Christ consists of many diverse members, so when those who have intellectual gifts speak they should do so as one part, and not the most important part, of larger Christian communities. Once again, this volume offers many examples of such. Further, when we do express our concerns intellectually, we need to be looking for common ground in our common humanity with those with whom we differ. What we do is not going to change the whole world or nearly the whole of our culture. Yet, as this volume illustrates, collectively it can have a substantial impact.

Acknowledgments

One of the most gratifying parts of completing a book, especially a book with as many kind and thoughtful contributors as this one, is thanking everyone who played a part in its development.

Long before this book began, Indiana Wesleyan University's president, David W. Wright, and provost, Stacy Hammons, entrusted us with the responsibility of developing the Lumen Research Institute. In partnership with friends at Excelsia College in Macquarie Park, New South Wales, Lumen has since emerged as "a global collective of Christian scholars who pursue questions of social concern through collaborative and interdisciplinary research efforts" (as its mission states).

Together, we then led the State of the Evangelical Mind project and now the Public Intellectuals and the Common Good project. As we finish this second project, we are preparing to launch our third, Mentoring Matters. Hopefully, these projects laid the foundation for a scholarly institute worthy of passing along to the next generation of scholars.

We are fortunate to call Jack Gardner, proprietor of Jax Café, in Marion, Indiana, a friend who always kept the coffee brewing when inspiration was running low. If he was ever frustrated by our loitering, he seemingly offered nothing but hospitality. The ideas that led to this book, its predecessor, and its successor were all developed at Jax.

We benefited greatly from Erin Drummy's keen research skills and critical eye. She partnered with us on the chapter in the *Higher Education Handbook* that then laid the foundation for this volume. By the time these words are published, unfortunately (*at least selfishly speaking, for us*), Erin will have graduated from Taylor University. In the near future, a graduate program and the community it fosters will be fortunate to welcome her as one of its newest members.

Over the years, Jon Boyd with InterVarsity Press has become someone whose value as an editor is superseded only by his value as a friend. While he is honest enough to call us out on our less than inspired ideas, he is gracious enough to encourage us on our decent ones. In his capable editorial hands, we entrusted those decent ones, knowing that in time those ideas would be worthy of sharing with others.

Indianapolis's Sagamore Institute has now become a home away from home where we have met to test these ideas through the symposia we have hosted. Sagamore's president, Jay Hein, and fellows such as Donald Cassell continue to cultivate an international reputation for the institute's commitment to the heartland. While Anne Raway, Sagamore's operations manager, may relish her role behind the scenes, we all know she's the one who truly makes things happen at Sagamore.

We want to thank all of the contributors to this volume and the symposium at Sagamore that preceded it—Miroslav Volf, Amos Yong, Heather Templeton Dill, Linda A. Livingstone, Katelyn Beaty, Father Emmanuel Katongole, and John M. Perkins. We were truly fortunate to work with such brilliant and gracious people. We are hopeful you also find their ideas to be what makes this volume worthy of your time and consideration.

Finally, we want to thank George M. Marsden for his willingness to offer the foreword for this volume. In many ways, he epitomizes the virtues of a Christian scholar. As with so many, *The Soul of the American University* was critical to our formation. Having his words included in this volume is thus an honor.

Introduction

Todd C. Ream, Jerry Pattengale, and Christopher J. Devers

Shortly after the turn of the millennium, in the February 2, 2001, issue of *The Chronicle of Higher Education*, University of Notre Dame president emeritus Theodore M. Hesburgh, CSC, asked, "Where Are College Presidents' Voices on Important Public Issues?"[1] He noted in that essay that scholars and, in particular, college presidents had abandoned questions plaguing the public.

Hesburgh argued that the pressure to raise funds drove college presidents to embrace politically safer ground than wading into the uncertainty that can come with public engagement. As a former member and chair of the federal Civil Rights Commission, he argued that the most pressing issues of the day were being decided in arenas void of individuals who were arguably best trained to provide the needed insights.

Little has changed since Hesburgh made that argument. Books and articles concerning public intellectuals generally begin with the assumption that their contributions are valuable but relatively absent, at least in Western culture. As a result, some of the most recent additions to the literature draw insights from practices public intellectuals embrace within a global context.

---

[1] Theodore M. Hesburgh, CSC, "Where Are College Presidents' Voices on Important Public Issues?," *Chronicle of Higher Education*, February 1, 2001, https://news.nd.edu/news/where-are-college-presidents-voices-on-important-public-issues.

Although history notes the prominent role evangelical intellectuals once played in Western culture, history also records their relative absence. As Mark A. Noll chronicled in 1995 in *The Scandal of the Evangelical Mind,* part of the challenge was the relative lack of evangelicals' intellectual engagement. By nearly every known indicator, intellectual engagement among evangelicals has increased since that time. However, evangelicals are not immune to the lure of political safety or the perils of specialization. The scholarship they produce all too often fails to inform a particular public, whether that public be the church or the state, or both.

This volume includes essays by eminent scholars and practitioners addressing those issues. It emerged from a larger project by the same name that began with a symposium held at the Sagamore Institute in Indianapolis in September 2019. This project was defined by attempts to answer questions in the present context such as: What would a commitment to the common good look like when exercised by evangelical scholars? What historically well-defined qualities of public intellectuals need to be adopted? What qualities need to be jettisoned? What ones might need to be cultivated anew?

To answer those questions, that project sought to assess the present array of challenges, identify valuable opportunities, and provide examples of relevant practices as they relate to helping evangelical scholars expand their vocational understanding to include that of the public intellectual. Far from where some self-appointed public intellectuals find themselves working today, this project also sought to help evangelical scholars cultivate a sense of need for their work in relation to the common good.

To contextualize those efforts as represented by the contributions included in this volume, what immediately follows includes (1) a discussion of the impact the current divisive culture has on evangelicals in general and evangelical scholars in particular, (2) an attempt to define the phrase *public intellectual* along with an assessment of the challenges those individuals face, and (3) an attempt to define the phrase *common good* along with an argument for its value within the Christian tradition.

"Am I My Brother's Keeper?"

Amid the challenges posed by COVID-19, the debates that defined the 2020 presidential election were the latest installments in waves of increasing incivility. Debates in fall 2019 and winter 2020 on whether to impeach President Donald Trump, the autumn 2018 confirmation hearing of now–Supreme Court Justice Brett Kavanaugh, and the 2016 presidential election are but a few expressions of partisanship-defined incivility. Those expressions are not limited to professional politicians in Washington, DC; they plague local politics as well as professional and personal affairs of almost every kind.

A burgeoning array of titles now seeks to define such incivility, deduce its origins, and chart a course that may transcend it.[2] Perhaps the most insightful of those titles is Ezra Klein's *Why We're Polarized*. In particular, Klein notes, "Everyone engaged in American politics is engaged in identity politics," and "those identities are most powerful when they are so pervasive as to be either invisible or uncontroversial."[3] Perhaps even more disturbing is that people are identifying with growing intensity with which group they are not a

---

[2]For example, consider titles such as James E. Campbell, *Polarized: Making Sense of a Divided America* (Princeton, NJ: Princeton University Press, 2016); Kenneth J. Collins, *Power, Politics and the Fragmentation of Evangelicalism: From the Scopes Trial to the Obama Administration* (Downers Grove, IL: InterVarsity Press, 2012); Nolan McCarty, *Polarization: What Everyone Needs to Know* (New York: Oxford University Press, 2019); and Thomas Carothers and Andrew O'Donohue, eds., *Democracies Divided: The Global Challenge of Political Polarization* (Washington, DC: Brookings Institution Press, 2019).

[3]Ezra Klein, *Why We're Polarized* (New York: Avid Reader, 2020), xx-xxii.

part, not which group they are a part. In simple terms, identity is growing stronger based on one not being a Democrat versus one being a Republican and vice versa.

What is newly occurring is "that our political identities are changing—and strengthening" while they are also subdividing. As a result, Klein contends, "Over the past fifty years, our partisan identities have merged with our racial, religious, geographic, ideological, and cultural identities. Those merged identities have attained a weight that is breaking our institutions and tearing at the bonds that hold this country together." While those challenges are evident in politics, Klein also contends that one other place they are immediately evident is where most public intellectuals do their work— college and university campuses, which Klein contends are "hothouse atmosphere[s] where fights take place with particular clarity; as the moderating forces of non-college life—keeping your job, barely having time to go to the gym much less to political protests— are lifted."[4]

Perhaps what belies this contentious nature of this polarized culture, regardless of where it may exist, is this: as a result of the fear that we are truly alone, human beings slake their thirst at the trough of tribalism only to discover they are ingesting nothing but sand at the bottom of a mirage. In such an age, we may no longer know who we are, but we seek solace in knowing we are not the ones we label as our enemies.

If we are even remotely correct in identifying what drives such incivility, we should then not be surprised that such a problem has plagued humanity since the events recorded Genesis 4:9: "Then the LORD said to Cain, 'Where is your brother Abel?' 'I don't know,'" he

---

[4]Klein, *Why We're Polarized*, xxii-xxiii, 126.

replied. 'Am I my brother's keeper?'" (NIV). The verses preceding this exchange note that Abel brought "fat portions from some of the firstborn of his flock" as an offering for the Lord while Cain "brought some of the fruits of the soil" (NIV) as his offering. The Lord found favor with Abel's offering but not with Cain's.

In Genesis 4:6, the Lord asks Cain, "Why are you angry? Why is your face downcast? If you do what is right, will you not be accepted? But if you do not do what is right, sin is crouching at your door; it desires to have you, but you must rule over it" (NIV). Cain neither offers a response to the Lord's question nor heeds the Lord's warning. Instead, Cain lures Abel out into a field, where Cain kills his brother.

When the Lord then asks, "Where is your brother Abel?" Cain famously answers that he does not know and asks, "Am I my brother's keeper?"—a query that harbors both moral and ontological overtones. On one level, Cain asks whether he is morally responsible for his brother. On another level, he asks whether his identity is ontologically related to that of his brother. Both the Lord and Abel respond affirmatively to that question and its multilayered meaning. The Lord speaks, demanding that Cain heed Abel's response, "What have you done? Listen! Your brother's blood cries out to me from the ground" (Genesis 4:10 NIV). In essence, the Lord contends Cain is morally responsible for and ontologically defined by the relationship he shared with Abel.

What makes human beings like God is their capacity and even need to make meaning. When human beings morally and ontologically divorce themselves from one another, they succumb to being something less than that for which they were created. Instead of their identity first being rooted in what they share in common with others, their identity becomes rooted in contradistinction to individuals with whom they believe they share in common little to nothing. In essence, they ask, "Am I my brother's keeper?"

Something within human beings knows their identity and in turn that their responsibility is never truly to themselves. The false security of tribalism and, in particular, identity based on with which tribe one does *not* identify, however, becomes a temptation that proves difficult to resist. History is thus littered with accounts of how the narrative of Cain and Abel has replayed itself on both small and large scales.

Space does not allow us to trace even a fraction of ways Cain's question has been asked over time. For the sake of our specific efforts, we will skip to New Haven, Connecticut, in 1943. Along with his wife, Raïssa, Jacques Maritain fled his native France during World War II and eventually found himself delivering the Terry Lectures at Yale University, published by Yale University Press under the title *Education at the Crossroads*.

The heart of Maritain's argument is that the Christian humanism that should define educational aspirations was all but vanquished in Europe and was under assault in the United States. If asked, Maritain would likely have contended that Cain was ontologically tied to and thus morally responsible for Abel. In *The Year of Our Lord 1943: Christian Humanism in an Age of Crisis*, Alan Jacobs summarized Maritain's argument:

> Though intuition and love cannot be taught directly, it is the task of the teacher to help form young people so that when the opportunity comes, outside of school, for them to acquire intuition and love, they will be prepared to do so. Teachers, then, play a pivotal role in the building and sustaining of meaningful human culture: if they do not intervene in young people's lives,

in the indirect yet distinctive ways that only they can, the culture will surely, if slowly fall.

In essence, human beings are defined by the quality of relationships they share with one another. Maritain and his wife had fled a Europe being torn apart by the moral and ontological mirages offered by tribalism. As a result of the formative role teachers are called to serve, Maritain wanted to encourage them to cultivate habits in their students that would lead to the "building and sustaining of a meaningful human culture."[5]

A little more than ten years after Maritain, Romano Guardini wrote *The End of the Modern World*. In particular, Guardini believed that power and, in particular, its misuse had contributed to the tribalism the world had witnessed. Guardini does not argue power is inherently sinful. In contrast, he contends that only when "man's natural God-likeness consists in this capacity for power, in his ability to use it and his resultant lordship . . . does the phenomenon of power receive its full weight, its greatness, as well as its earnestness, which is grounded in responsibility." Reminiscent of the Lord's question to Cain, Guardini then offers, "Man is lord by the grace of God, and he must exercise his dominion responsibly, for he is answerable for it to him who is Lord by essence."[6]

George Marsden, when looking back at the 1950s in the United States, has seen signs of the realities that compelled Maritain and Guardini to issue their warnings. In *The Twilight of the American Enlightenment: The 1950s and the Crisis of Liberal Belief*, Marsden argues that what was "fascinating and revealing" about midcentury America was "how easily talk about the unassailable ideal of 'freedom'

---

[5]Alan Jacobs, *The Year of Our Lord 1943: Christian Humanism in an Age of Crisis* (New York: Oxford University Press, 2018), 127.
[6]Romano Guardini, *The End of the Modern World* (Wilmington, DE: ISI Books, 1998), 133-34.

in a political sense blended into an ideal of personal attitudes of independence from so-called social authorities and restraints. A key word that was of often used to express this taken-for-granted ideal was 'autonomy.'" In essence, if autonomy was an ideal to which one should aspire, what moral and ontological relationship did one then share with others? Marsden notes that the opposite of autonomy in the fifties was perceived to be conformity, and "everyone, it seemed, agreed that one should not be a conformist."[7] Part of the genius in Marsden's assessment is his acknowledging that seeds of the cultural expressions found to be widespread in the late 1960s and early 1970s were well planted by the 1950s.

Challenges to the moral and ontological relationships that humans share are represented in sociological realities notably articulated by Robert Putnam in *Bowling Alone: The Collapse and Revival of American Community*. As the title creatively posits, people traditionally bowled in leagues as recreational yet substantive expressions of the communal relations they shared. But in recent decades, they bowl alone. Autonomy, when prized, not only fails to see the need for such relations but even eschews them. The demise of such relations, however, is not limited to recreational experiences such as bowling. Civic organizations such as the Parent Teacher Association, Lions Club, Kiwanis, and Shriners also have seen declines in participation.

Although Putnam is concerned with the viability of such organizations, he is at least equally concerned with what they facilitate when it comes to what sociologists refer to as social capital. In essence, he wants to know "how the positive consequences of social capital—mutual support, cooperation, trust, institutional effectiveness—can be maximized and the negative manifestations—sectarianism,

---

[7]George M. Marsden, *The Twilight of the American Enlightenment: The 1950s and the Crisis of Liberal Belief* (New York: Basic Books, 2014), 23.

ethnocentrism, corruption—minimized."[8] Putman understands that humans are essentially relational beings who were going to forge associations with others in either constructive or destructive ways. In essence, there is a fine yet significant line between mutual support and sectarianism.

Having witnessed the growing propensity for people to bowl alone, Hesburgh offered in 2011 that "we remain a divided nation," and that "incivility has again crept into our society and raised its ugly head in a way that threatens the fabric of American life." As if he were anticipating the temper of the 2016 presidential election, Hesburgh then contended, "Incivility seems to have gained social acceptance at a time when we should be at relative peace, working together to move into the twenty-first century." Evidence of such behavior, according to Hesburgh, is found in the fact that "many of us are shouting at others, and even more of us are shouting just for the sake of shouting on the Internet, in newspaper columns, in political ads, on talk radio, at the stop light, at the dinner table, at the negotiating table, in the halls of high school and in the halls of Congress."[9] Divorced from being one another's keepers, we manifest misappropriated social capital in the myriad ways incivility is now expressed.

Evangelical Scholars in an Age of Incivility

When trying to ascertain how evangelicalism can find its way in an age of incivility, insights yielded by historians again prove helpful. One curiosity of the 2016 presidential election was that evangelicals, in particular white evangelicals, voted for Donald Trump at higher rates than any previous candidate for which comparable data was

---

[8]Robert D. Putnam, *Bowling Alone: The Collapse and Revival of American Community* (New York: Simon & Schuster, 2000), 22.
[9]Theodore M. Hesburgh, introduction to *Civility in America: Essays from America's Thought Leaders* (New York: DGI, 2011), 6-8.

available. Seeking to come to terms with that reality, John Fea offers *Believe Me: The Evangelical Road to Donald Trump*. Fea's explanation does not reside merely with events occurring over the course of the weeks or even months leading up to the 2016 election. In fact, Fea argues that what took place that fall was drawn from a "political playbook [that] was written in the 1970s and drew from an even longer history of white evangelical fear."[10]

Such a playbook, according to Fea, is "grounded in a highly problematic interpretation of the relationship between Christianity and the American founding." Fea was not surprised to find that "playbook [being one] that too often gravitates toward nativism, xenophobia, racism, intolerance, and an unbiblical view of American exceptionalism." In summary, Fea believes that "it is a playbook that divides rather than unites."[11]

What put that playbook back into circulation, Fea contends, was that evangelicals found themselves at the mercy of political forces— one emanating from the left and one from the right. From the left, Fea proposes, "Having found its footing on the progressive side of the same-sex marriage issue, the Obama administration became relentless in its advocacy of social policies that not only made traditional evangelicals cringe but also infused them with a sense of righteous anger." From the right, "Fears of rapid moral decline would seem like unpromising moral territory for Donald Trump to work," but Trump "was a quick learner."[12] Over time, Trump capitalized on the narrative of fear to which evangelicals found themselves subscribing by telling them who was to blame for it. Regardless of whatever misgivings evangelicals had about seeing Trump in the White House, they were

---

[10]John Fea, *Believe Me: The Evangelical Road to Donald Trump* (Grand Rapids: Eerdmans, 2018), 6.

[11]Fea, *Believe Me*, 6-7.

[12]Fea, *Believe Me*, 27-29.

eclipsed by thoughts of Barack Obama's heir apparent, Hillary Clinton, taking up residence once again on Pennsylvania Avenue.

By the time Thomas S. Kidd published *Who Is an Evangelical?* in 2019, the potentially apt subtitle accompanying his book read *The History of a Movement in Crisis*. Kidd opens by referencing the 2016 election and the historic support Trump received from white evangelicals. While Kidd then reaches further back into history than Fea, he concludes by trying to address a comparable set of questions and comes to some comparable conclusions. In particular, Kidd acknowledges that "the damage caused by evangelical white voters for Trump was substantial, leading many women and people of color to question the fundamental integrity of the [evangelical] movement." As a result, Kidd notes, "In the aftermath of the election, stories proliferated about blacks, Hispanics, and other people leaving evangelical churches and dropping the evangelical label."[13]

Kidd, however, is not inclined to drop that label. He may believe the movement is in crisis, but all is not lost. Although that crisis "resulted from the widespread perception that the movement is primarily about obtaining power within the Republican party," what defines evangelicalism is much greater than what those efforts reveal. For example, Kidd is quick to point out that "everywhere you look on the charitable landscape, evangelicals are there," citing the efforts of vast networks of organizations, large, small, and everywhere in between to be the hands and feet of Christ.[14] He thus views the 2016 election as a cautionary tale concerning what can happen when Christians become too closely associated with the political machinery on one side of the aisle or the other.

---

[13]Thomas S. Kidd, *Who Is an Evangelical?: The History of a Movement in Crisis* (New Haven, CT: Yale University Press, 2019), 149.
[14]Kidd, *Who Is an Evangelical?*, 152, 154.

Mark Noll, David Bebbington, and George M. Marsden offer a context for comparable questions to be addressed in their edited volume *Evangelicals: Who They Have Been, Are Now, and Could Be.* Like Fea and Kidd, Noll opens the introduction by noting, "The word 'evangelical' is in trouble—but for different and competing reasons." Specifically, Noll mentions three. First, Noll acknowledges, "Pollsters and pundits have fixated on the overwhelming support [Donald Trump] has received from a constituency often called simply 'evangelicals'—or, if there is a pause for breath, 'white evangelicals.'"[15]

Second, Noll argues that a critical while perhaps less obvious component in these discussions involves divisions between historians concerning how the story of evangelicalism is told. *Evangelicalism* remains a difficult term to define. While some definitions have gained more support than others, Noll's up-to-date survey of the literature points out that defining what one means by *evangelical* is a far-from-settled matter. As a result, a host of questions persist. For example, What Christian traditions within Protestantism and now even within Catholicism might aptly be labeled as evangelical? Or what historically African American traditions might appropriately be considered evangelical?

Finally, Noll offers that even if a consensus existed concerning how a term such as *evangelical* is defined within the United States, such a definition may not prove true in other parts of the world. In particular, he notes that what emerges does not involve "political or theological standoffs" but "sheer, mind-boggling diversity."[16] The questions noted in the preceding paragraph about what traditions within Christianity might be included within evangelicalism grow

---

[15]Mark A. Noll, introduction to *Evangelicals: Who They Have Been, Are Now, and Could Be,* ed. Mark A Noll, David W. Bebbington, and George M. Marsden (Grand Rapids: Eerdmans, 2019), 1-2.

[16]Noll, introduction to *Evangelicals,* 11.

exponentially when extended beyond North America. Compounding those challenges is that many labels, especially sociological, that apply in North America do not describe realities elsewhere. One cannot assume that identifying characteristics of an evangelical in one region of the world are applicable—or inapplicable—in another. Evangelicalism, in essence, is thus most aptly appreciated in its full complexity.

Into this mix of incivility in the wider culture and the crisis within evangelicalism are Christian scholars seeking to fulfill their calling. We note that few, if any, of them have found themselves free from these challenges. Writing about his own faith journey in *The Second Mountain: The Quest for a Moral Life*, David Brooks proposes that for individuals wrestling with their faith, "Religious people and institutions sometimes built ramps that made it easier to continue my journey, or they built walls, making the journey harder." In relation to the construction of walls, Brooks contends that they "were caused by the combination of an intellectual inferiority complex combined with a spiritual superiority complex."[17]

We look at a couple of those walls if for no other reason than they lure evangelical scholars away from fulfilling their vocations. In particular, Brooks notes that Christians can slip into "siege mentality" and seek ways to withdraw "into the purity of [an] enclave." Doing so is comforting to many, "as it gives people a straightforward way to interpret the world—the noble us versus the powerful and sinful them."[18] Such an inclination is understandable, given the previously detailed challenges facing evangelicalism and the wider culture. The problem is that it promotes "pathological dualism" and impairs the

---

[17]David Brooks, *The Second Mountain: The Quest for a Moral Life* (New York: Random House, 2019), 256.

[18]Brooks, *Second Mountain*, 256.

ability or perhaps even the willingness of individuals within an enclave to listen to others beyond it. As a result, do evangelical scholars read writers who reinforce their own beliefs? Or do they read both people who support and who challenge them?

Brooks also notes that within the false security of an enclave, "intellectual mediocrity" can plague the efforts of Christian scholars. Referencing his experience at Yale University, Brooks contends his colleagues "are brutal. But they are brutal in search of excellence." Being brutal may not be the only route to excellence, but his criticism that Christians within their own communities "want to be nice; they want to be affirming, and that softens all discussion" merits consideration. In the end, softening discussion to the point of being dishonest does not serve anyone well. In addition, allowing mediocrity to parade as a worthy return on the sacrifice Christ made is sacrilege. In Brooks's estimation, the story Mark Noll traced in his previously mentioned *Scandal* "is still ongoing," but with "some notable exceptions."[19]

The Peril (and the Promise) of Public Intellectuals

With some notable exceptions, one should not think the circumstances facing scholars in general and public intellectuals in particular are without challenges. As with Noll's, Brooks's criticisms have merit and deserve the serious consideration of evangelical scholars. Scholars serving in many institutional contexts have found themselves contending with the conditions perpetuated by a culture of rising incivility. The higher the profile of the scholar, the more likely that scholar has experienced those challenges. Public intellectuals are needed in both the church and society, and serving in such a capacity increases one's exposure.

---

[19]Brooks, *Second Mountain*, 257.

To come to terms with what defines a public intellectual, Michael Desch, editor of *Public Intellectuals in the Global Arena: Professors or Pundits?*, offers a concise definition: public intellectuals are "persons who exert a large influence in the contemporary society of their country of origin through their thought, writing, or speaking."[20] Such individuals often but not always hold academic appointments. Some public intellectuals serve think tanks, others in capacities such as journalism. Regardless, they exert a significant influence through their thought, writing, and speaking, within the context of a particular public. Although persons holding academic appointments may be prolific scholars within their particular field, they would not be considered public intellectuals if their work did not have appeal to and among some sector of the wider society.

A growing number of titles has focused on the importance of public intellectuals while also noting the challenges they face. A sample of that list of titles includes words such as *endangered, last, anxious,* and even *death.*[21] Perhaps the most widely recognized of those titles is Richard Posner's *Public Intellectuals: A Study of Decline.* In particular, Posner notes that a "striking variance [exists] in the quality of public-intellectual work, coupled with a low average quality—low and maybe falling, though it would be more precise to say that public-intellectual work is becoming less distinctive, less interesting, and less important."[22]

---

[20]Michael C. Desch, introduction to *Public Intellectuals in the Global Arena: Professors or Pundits?*, ed. Michael C. Desch (Notre Dame, IN: University of Notre Dame Press, 2016), 1.
[21]For example, see Amatai Etzioni and Alyssa Bowditch, eds., *Public Intellectuals: An Endangered Species?* (Lanham, MD: Rowman & Littlefield, 2006); Russell Jacoby, *The Last Intellectuals: American Culture in the Age of Academe* (New York: Basic Books, 2000); John Michael, *Anxious Intellects: Academic Professionals, Public Intellectuals, and Enlightenment Values* (Durham, NC: Duke University Press, 2000); and Thomas M. Nichols, *The Death of Expertise: The Campaign Against Established Knowledge and Why It Matters* (New York: Oxford University Press, 2017).
[22]Richard Posner, *Public Intellectuals: A Study in Decline* (Cambridge, MA: Harvard University Press, 2001), 2-3.

Part of the problem, according to Posner, is that today "the typical public intellectual is a safe specialist." As a result, he or she "is not the type of person well suited to play the public intellectual's most distinctive, though not only, role, that of a critical commentator addressing a non-specialist audience on matters of broad public concern."[23]

In *The Last Intellectuals: American Culture in the Age of Academe*, Russell Jacoby offers a related yet different take on the problem. In particular, he argues that younger scholars poised to serve as public intellectuals may not even see the need to do so. "Younger intellectuals no longer need or want a larger public; they are almost exclusively professors. Campuses are their homes; colleagues their audience, monographs and specialized journals their media." However, Jacoby notes this generation of scholars is not entirely to blame, as "their jobs, advancement, and salaries depend on the evaluation of specialists."[24] By virtue of their training, younger scholars may not be well suited to serve as public intellectuals. Furthermore, the reward structures surrounding them may not even acknowledge such efforts as being of value.

Finally, Jean Bethke Elshtain offers a view that transcends both the challenges posed by the training received by intellectuals and the culture in which they operate. In particular, Elshtain's concern stems from "the triumph of a generally secular, consumerist worldview, and with mainline Protestantism's abandonment of much of its own intellectual tradition in favor of a therapeutic ethos."[25] Elshtain packs more into that observation than space will allow for full consideration. One could argue, for example, that the need to be nice that Brooks references in relation to the intellectual life of evangelicals is the result of a residue left by that therapeutic ethos stemming from mainline Protestantism.

---

[23]Posner, *Public Intellectuals*, 5.
[24]Jacoby, *Last Intellectuals*, 6.
[25]Jean Bethke Elshtain, "Why Public Intellectuals?," in Etzioni and Bowditch, *Public Intellectuals*, 84.

A more limited focus settles on the fact as a result of secularism "there is no longer a unified culture to address—or to rebel against." According to Elshtain, proponents of one view or another resort to promoting "a sense of self-importance by exaggerating what one is ostensibly up against."[26] Such efforts, often collapsing into shrill exercises in which even ad hominem arguments may no longer be viewed as fallacious, point to the possibility that efforts made by public intellectuals are no longer defined by a clear purpose or end.

Toward a Beatific Vision of the Common Good

Perhaps one purpose or end for the efforts made by public intellectuals, however, is offered by the common good. Such an understanding has a long history in Western culture and in variant forms around the world. Such an understanding is also seeing a resurgence, at least in the literature. In relation to higher education alone, Jason Owen-Smith published *Research Universities and the Public Good: Discoveries for an Uncertain Future* with Stanford University Press in 2018, and in 2019 Charles Dorn published *For the Common Good: A New History of Higher Education* with Cornell University Press. In the prologue, Dorn acknowledges the criticism higher education has received in recent years—even going so far as to launch his defense with, "Higher education in America is against the ropes." In response, Dorn contends colleges and universities opened their doors in decades and centuries past by claiming to promote "the common good as a principal aim." The void Dorn seeks to fill is that "we know surprisingly little about how colleges and universities have achieved it over time, if at all."[27]

---

[26]Elshtain, "Why Public Intellectuals?," 84.
[27]Charles Dorn, *For the Common Good: A History of Higher Education in America* (Ithaca, NY: Cornell University Press, 2019), 1-2.

Such contributions are not limited to higher education. From both sides of the Atlantic, arguments have also emerged concerning the value the common good offers society as a whole. For example, in 2019 Polity published a series of conversations between Peter Engelmann and Alain Badiou. As an extension of Badiou's previously explicated commitments, those pages include a defense of the value of the common good from a Marxist perspective. In particular, Badiou looks for evidence of a society's response to questions such as, "How do we ensure that everyone has enough to eat? How do we ensure everyone receives the necessary training? How do we ensure the sick all receive the necessary medication? How do we ensure that everyone can travel unhindered from one place to another?"[28]

Robert B. Reich's *The Common Good* was published in 2018. In contrast to Badiou's Marxism, Reich sees the justification for an emphasis on the common good as emanating from political pragmatism. As a result, Reich's belief in the ability of the common good to meet the needs of the greatest number of people is defined in a scenario he poses about what occurs in its absence:

> We depend upon people's widespread and voluntary willingness to abide by laws—not just the literal letter of the law but also the spirit and intent of them. Consider what would happen if no one voluntarily obeyed the law without first calculating what they could gain by violating it as compared with the odds of the violation being discovered multiplied by the size of the likely penalty. We'd be living in bedlam.[29]

In essence, the value of the common good is evident in the way it works.

---

[28]Alain Badiou and Peter Englemann, *For a Politics of a Common Good*, trans. Wieland Hoban (Medford, MA: Polity, 2019), 90.

[29]Robert B. Reich, *The Common Good* (New York: Knopf, 2018), 22.

Christian theologians have also made valuable contributions to this discussion. For example, 2019 witnessed the publication of Jake Meador's *In Search of the Common Good: Christian Fidelity in a Fractured World* and Jonathan Wilson-Hartgrove's *Revolution of Values: Reclaiming Public Faith for the Common Good*, both released by InterVarsity Press; Daniela C. Augustine published *The Spirit and the Common Good: Shared Flourishing in the Image of God* with Eerdmans. Augustine's particular work argues for what she identifies as a pneumatological anthropology and that "the path toward attaining the likeness of God demands cooperation and alignment of the free human will with the divine will."[30] In essence, human flourishing is the result of the relationship members of the Trinity share with one another and, in turn, the relations humans have a chance to share with one another. To support her argument, Augustine turns to insights from a number of Christian traditions but wisely places a considerable emphasis on what the Eastern Orthodox tradition offers.

We see an additional argument for the common good coming from the Catholic tradition in the work of Jacques Maritain in *The Person and the Common Good*. This slim volume, based in part on lectures Maritain gave beginning in 1939, was first published in the United States in 1947. Comparable to Augustine's argument, Maritain offers that before humans "are related to the immanent common good of the universe, they are related to an infinitely greater good—the separated common Good, the divine transcendent Whole."[31] Risking oversimplification, human flourishing is contingent on the web of relations they initiate that, in their origins, extend from the

---

[30]Daniela C. Augustine, *The Spirit and the Common Good* (Grand Rapids: Eerdmans, 2019), 18.
[31]Jacques Maritain, *The Person and the Common Good* (Notre Dame, IN: University of Notre Dame Press, 1966), 18.

web of relations shared by members of the Trinity. In essence, the common good is not defined first and foremost by what works but by the way it reflects the very character of God.

Maritain continues to argue that such relations change how we see. However imperfect that line of sight might be this side of eternity, humans come to see the world via what Thomas Aquinas and, in turn, Maritain refer to as a beatific vision, or "the supremely personal act by which the soul, transcending absolutely every sort of created common good, enters into the very bliss of God and draws life from the uncreated Good, the divine essence itself, the uncreated common Good of three divine Persons."[32]

Risking oversimplification once again, the common within creation is a reflection of the perfect relations shared by the uncreated common good of the Trinity. By virtue of the beatific vision that grace makes possible, humans are then called to cultivate those relations this side of eternity.

How do we define the works public intellectuals pursue? We note their ability to mediate between God and humanity, the eternal and the temporal, the just and the unjust, through their thought, writing, or speaking. Such work is inherently interdisciplinary, as it begins and ends with glimpses offered to them by the beatific vision that, again, grace makes possible. Returning to the words of Hesburgh, "[Christ] alone mediates perfectly." Regardless, the "function of mediation looks both to God and to men: to God in worship and atonement for sin, the basis of disunity, and to men in order to bring them divine grace and truth in Christ, the center of unity."[33] Such a calling, a calling to the common good in which the public intellectual's vocation is defined, is an arduous one, but is also one for which grace proves sufficient.

---

[32]Maritain, *Person and the Common Good*, 21.
[33]Theodore M. Hesburgh, *The Theology of Catholic Action* (Notre Dame, IN: Ave Maria, 1946), 57.

Volume Overview

Such an understanding of the public intellectual's vocation merits much further explication, and the essays that follow begin that process. In part one, Miroslav Volf and Amos Yong offer their theological reflections on the relationship public intellectuals share with the common good. In part two, Linda Livingstone, Heather Templeton Dill, and Katelyn Beaty offer their thoughts on how such a relationship is cultivated from their respective vantage points as a university president, a foundation president, and a journalist. In part three, Emmanuel Katongole notes how his efforts to serve the common good as a public intellectual in turn affected his scholarship. This volume then closes with an interview conducted by David W. Wright with John M. Perkins about the ways Perkins has sought to be God's voice, hands, and feet this side of eternity.

The wisdom offered by this distinguished group of contributors, however, is just the beginning of a conversation the church, the university, and society need.

Part 1

Theological Reflections

1

On Being a Christian Public Intellectual

Miroslav Volf

We live in a time of disorienting change. Around the end of the twentieth century, many things we long took for granted about our common life started to become questionable. Institutions and practices in many domains of life are undergoing rapid transformations. That is partly because accelerating technological developments are transforming all domains of life, from what we wear to how we wage wars, from how we play to how we work. But the disorientation is tied also to our deep values, to the "gods" that legitimize and orient our action in public space. Our gods are at war with one another. As we watch them strut around with puffed-out chests, charge at each other, or stagger bruised and bloodied, we are not sure which ones will be left standing.

To negotiate all these changes, we need at least three things: (1) to understand the seemingly chaotic world around us; (2) to discern, articulate, and commend visions of the good, flourishing life in diverse and largely pluralistic contexts; and (3) to find navigable paths to reach together the goals aligned with those visions. All three requirements are daunting. We can grapple with none of them without the help of public intellectuals, those among the knowledge workers who address matters of common concern and whose intended audience is the larger public.

Understanding Our World

Consider changes in four significant domains of our lives: environment, economy, politics, and cultural imagination about the character of humanity. The four domains are interconnected, but I will have to leave these enmeshments aside here and concentrate on the distinct challenges in each.

Environment. The kind of modernization our major institutions are all designed to serve, and with which most humans today strongly identify, is proving unsustainable. The most basic reason is, as Bruno Latour puts it, the "lack of a planet vast enough" to accommodate the dream of rapid and unending expansion that propels modernization.[1] Earth's ecosystem is straining to withstand human assault and is hitting back in the form of extreme weather events, for instance. In response, some, mostly the superrich and techno-geeks, are laying the foundations of a possible escape into paradisiac space colonies; others, mostly the poor and religious, are counting on the second coming to rapture them out of the coming desolation. The challenge before us is to rediscover a vision of a shared world as the home for the entire community of creation.

Economics. It is hard to miss the scandalously yawning gap between a small group of the superrich and the vast sea of the ultrapoor, both within and among the nations. But with regard to wealth generation, a bigger challenge than crass inequality may turn out to be the violence, oppression, and exploitation that the current world

---

[1] Bruno Latour, *Down to Earth: Politics in the New Climactic Regime*, trans. Catherine Porter (Cambridge, UK: Polity, 2018), 22.

economic system seems to require for no greater return than marginally lowering the cost of comfort for the growing middle class. One of the crassest examples of this is the violence against children and women in the Democratic Republic of the Congo driven by the search for profits from coltan, cobalt, and gold. It is not clear that such violence would diminish if the ultrarich gave away 90 percent of their wealth. Other troubling features of the finance-dominated current phase of capitalism are less obvious, perhaps, but deeply disconcerting, partly because they are at the root of both unconscionable wealth differentials and the violence toward the poorest of the poor.[2] For instance, this form of capitalism encourages a kind of social bond–dissolving meritocratic imagination that turns out to be nothing more than a sham.[3] It also seduces us to sever our idea of wealth from any connection with the entirety of the goods of creation, tangible and intangible, created or made, possessed individually or in common.[4]

Politics. Nationalisms are burgeoning everywhere; bridges between communities and nations are collapsing and walls are going up, all in the name of cultural, ethnic, or national identities defined in highly oppositional terms.[5] At the same time, the practice of democracy is rapidly losing legitimacy. Citizens in nations with long democratic traditions, such as the United States, no longer act as "partners in self-government." Instead, politics are "a form of war,"[6]

---

[2]For a comprehensive treatment, see Kathryn Tanner, *Christianity and the New Spirit of Capitalism* (New Haven, CT: Yale University Press, 2019).

[3]See Daniel Markovits, *The Meritocracy Trap: How America's Foundational Myth Feeds Inequality, Dismantles the Middle Class, and Devours the Elite* (New York: Penguin, 2019).

[4]See Miroslav Volf and Ryan McAnnally-Linz, *Public Faith in Action: How to Think Carefully, Engage Wisely, and Vote with Integrity* (Grand Rapids: Brazos, 2016), 33.

[5]See Miroslav Volf, *Exclusion and Embrace*, 2nd rev. ed. (Nashville: Abingdon, 2019), xiii-xxiii.

[6]Ronald Dworkin, *Is Democracy Possible Here?: Principles for a New Political Debate* (Princeton, NJ: Princeton University Press, 2006), 1.

as Ronald Dworkin put it in 2006, before the American political scene turned into the mud pit of incivility and demagogy that it has become since Donald Trump rose to political power. Even worse, both the political right and the political left are in crisis. The plutocratic and populist new-right has all but swallowed the conservative movement that rested on a moral vision (a contested one, to be sure, but a moral vision nonetheless). The factions on the left seem to agree on little more than the need for more equitable distribution of benefits.

Humanity. With the privatization of the goods characteristic of modern societies, many seem to have lost a sense of what it would mean to live lives that are worthy of our humanity, however divergently construed those visions of humanity may be. We work for resources so we can each pursue our unique dreams, but those dreams are unstable because they depend on our fickle tastes, while the resources have a way of morphing from means to ends themselves. When it comes to living a life worthy of our humanity, we are like those among frustrated painters who are so obsessed with the quality of their tools that they never actually get to painting.[7] We seem to have forgotten *how* to be authentically human, having even lost the sense that there is such a thing as true humanity.

As it turns out, we are uncertain about not only the *how* of humanity, but the *what* of it as well. For one, on both the progressive left and the radical right, doubt is spreading about the very idea of a common humanity.[8] Many consider shared biological roots, shared

---

[7] I owe the image to Hartmut Rosa, "Two Versions of the Good Life and Two Forms of Fear: Dynamic Stabilization and Resonance Conception of the Good Life" (paper presented at the Yale Center for Faith and Culture Consultation on Joy, Security, and Fear, New Haven, CT, November 8-9, 2017), 6.

[8] On the *what* (human essence) and the *how* of our humanity (fundamental orientation in life), see David Kelsey, *Eccentric Existence: A Theological Anthropology* (Louisville: Westminster John Knox, 2009), 1:1-2. For a powerful call to reaffirm our common humanity, see Paul Gilroy's

language, shared customs or practices, shared territory—in a phrase, a shared social identity—to be ontologically and not merely epistemologically prior to common humanity.[9] Concurrently, advances in science and technology continue to generate questions about what kind of a being a human is and who counts as one. Where are the lines separating humans from other animals on the one side and from likely future cybernetic "organisms" on the other?

The fundamental questions we face over our humanity, politics, economics, and environment cannot be addressed without rigorous scholarly work and deep reflection. Unless we adopt some form of nondemocratic authoritarianism as the preferred mode of governance, none of the answers that we may come up with will be embraced by citizens without what they consider to be compelling reasons. It will take public intellectuals to articulate and communicate these reasons. Public intellectuals are likely to be even more important in the future than they are today.

Two Challenges

Public intellectuals are indispensable, but today they face important, perhaps even unsurmountable, challenges. Let me name only two.

Gap between knowledge and opinion. The first challenge is to bridge the gap between reasonably established knowledge and popular opinion and, consequently, between scholars and the general public. Consider, first, the relation between public intellectuals and knowledge generators or scholars. We live in a time of specialized research and exponential growth of knowledge. As a

---

2019 Holberg Lecture, "Never Again: Refusing Race and Salvaging the Human," June 4, 2019, www.youtube.com/watch?v=Ta6UkmlXtVo. See also Jennifer A. Herdt, *Forming Humanity: Redeeming the German Bildung Tradition* (Chicago: University of Chicago Press, 2019).
[9]See, e.g., Alain de Benoist, *On Being a Pagan*, trans. John Graham (North Augusta, SC: Arcana Europa, 2018), 143.

result, we know a great deal about minute aspects of reality, but we are unsure how to organize this ever-growing knowledge into a unified whole. Given the astounding rates of knowledge production—knowledge is now said to be doubling roughly twice each day, and the rate is increasing exponentially—it seems impossible to pull highly specialized knowledge into the kind of unified vision needed to guide decision making in both personal and public domains.[10] It is just this impossible task that public intellectuals have to take on themselves. As a consequence, scholars often disdain public intellectuals as dilettantes. Those among scholars bold—or foolish—enough to wade into matters of common concern think of themselves often as amateurs in this task, their expertise in their own subfields notwithstanding.

The general public is often no more charitable to public intellectuals than is the scholarly community, perhaps for good reasons. Like scholars, but from a different perspective, the general population is scornful of public intellectuals' ignorance. Public intellectuals are too detached from life as it is lived on the ground; what they say or write may be correct in theory but is of no use in practice, as the saying goes, which was common already almost three centuries ago and to which Immanuel Kant took time to respond.[11]

When the wider public refuses to give public intellectuals respect and a hearing, public intellectuals lose their audience and, in an important sense, a dimension of their identity. Perhaps part of the

---

[10]In *Critical Path* (New York: St. Martin's, 1982), Buckminster Fuller proposes the "knowledge-doubling curve," an exponential increase in the rate of human knowledge. Up until 1900, human knowledge doubled about every century. By 1945, knowledge was doubling every twenty-five years, and by 1982 every twelve to thirteen months. An often-cited IBM report, "The Toxic Terabyte" (2006), states, "It is projected that just four years from now, the world's information base will be doubling in size every 11 hours."

[11]See Immanuel Kant, "On the Common Saying: That May Be Correct in Theory, but Is of No Use in Practice," in *Practical Philosophy* (Cambridge: Cambridge University Press, 1996), 277-309.

problem is that, though public intellectuals are eager to learn from scholars, they are, on the whole, not inclined to think (1) that the broader public has anything to teach them or (2) that having command of the vernacular matters.[12] But because the search for common goods is dialogical, it will have to involve paying attention not only to scholarly research but also to the wisdom of ordinary people living in concrete times and places.

Clashing moral universes. The first challenge facing public intellectuals is successful communication across an increasing chasm between scholarly knowledge and public opinion. The second challenge also concerns a chasm, not of knowledge but of moral vision and identity. Earlier, I mentioned a relatively recently formed divide between those who believe the earth is the single common home for all creatures to share and those who, marked by displaying scandalously self-centered exceptionalism, want to exit the earth and leave its denizens to face disaster. Another divide—many divides, in fact—concerns political differences, created after the French Revolution, between the left and the right on the trajectory of modernization and antimodernization.[13] Finally, the most ancient and enduring divides concern ethnic, racial, religious, and national identities.

Engaged in simmering or raging conflict across all these divides, participants get trapped in what they experience as alternative moral universes. That holds true for many public intellectuals as well. The more intense the struggles, the worse track record the intellectuals involved tend to have. In such situations, many become "reckless minds," to borrow a phrase from Mark Lilla's book on public

---

[12]Many public intellectuals today "have lost the command of the vernacular." Russell Jacoby, *The Last Intellectuals: American Culture in the Age of Academe* (New York: Basic Books, 2000), xv.

[13]For discussion of the three options mentioned above, see Latour, *Down to Earth*, 1-38.

intellectuals in twentieth-century Europe.[14] Celebrated philosophers, literary figures, and scientists who also acted as public intellectuals have been among the most ardent supporters of racism, colonialism, Nazism, Stalinism, and Maoism. In part this is because public intellectuals tend to identify too tightly with a group or ideology on one side of the trenches. An independent moral ground on which to stand is lost to them.

But it is not just that situations of moral and ideological conflicts generate and attract reckless minds. Such situations also tend to make inaudible and invisible those public intellectuals courageous enough to speak as independent moral agents. Split into blocs, the larger public loses ears to hear the voice speaking from a standpoint outside the moral binary defined by the struggle. Combatants on one side need those on the other side to be enemies, and those who assess the struggle from an independent standpoint and possibly offer mediating alternatives are shut out.[15]

Christian Public Intellectuals

What would it mean to be a Christian public intellectual in the setting in which public intellectuals are indispensable and find it a challenge to be both respected and heard?

Moral ground. The key question for any public intellectual—for any human being as well, of course—is the moral ground on which to stand. The temptation of a public intellectual is to pander to the

---

[14]Mark Lilla, *The Reckless Mind: Intellectuals in Politics*, rev. ed. (New York: New York Review of Books, 2016).

[15]On a small scale, this was my experience with *Exclusion and Embrace*. Its main theme, struggle over ethnic identity and possibilities of reconciliation, was informed to a significant degree by the war in former Yugoslavia in the 1990s. During the war, neither side found the book appealing. I was doing what combatants on both sides found highly annoying: I was judged to be humanizing their enemies and vilifying their friends. It found its readers, on both sides, after the war ended.

desires and interests of their own affinity groups. In ancient Greece, the so-called Sophists sought to acquire skill in rhetoric and debate so they could help political friends and harm enemies; they showed little concern for truth. Admittedly, this is how philosophers, notably Plato and Aristotle, describe the Sophists.[16] The philosophers' ideal was Socrates, a man for whom the search for truth stood above rhetorical skill and attachment to friends: "Never mind the manner, which may or may not be good; but think only of the truth of my words," Socrates said to the Athenians during his trial (in Plato's *Apology*). He was condemned to death because his attachment to truth brought him into opposition with the state and its gods.

Socrates was a philosopher and a public intellectual. It would be hard to call Jesus a public *intellectual*. Jesus spoke and acted publicly, and he was crucified for reasons not entirely dissimilar to those that led to Socrates's death sentence. But he was the Word-become-flesh and herald of the kingdom of God, of God's coming to dwell among the people of Israel and on the entire earth, more of a prophet than a critical thinker. Importantly—and, again, not entirely dissimilarly to Socrates—he did not only *speak* about God's coming to make the world into God's home; he also *embodied* the very vision he proclaimed. He was, as early church father Origen said of him, "God's kingdom itself." Conflict with religious and political rulers of the day got him crucified. But he was condemned to death under the auspice of a broader set of public institutions and agents, such as law and public opinion.[17]

For Christian public intellectuals, Socrates is a shining example of an intellectual radically committed to truth, but Jesus Christ, his

---

[16]See, e.g., among Plato's works: *Apology*, *Sophist*, *Statesman*, and *Theaetetus*.
[17]See Michael Welker, *God Revealed: Christology*, trans. Douglas W. Scott (Grand Rapids: Eerdmans, 2013), 192-97, 261.

teaching and his life, is the moral ground on which they stand. That moral ground is narrow and often uncomfortable—"the gate is narrow and the road is hard that leads to life, and there are few who find it" (Matthew 7:14)—but there are many legitimate ways to improvise it, depending on the changing situations in which Christians find themselves.[18] Still, the norm of anything Christian public intellectuals advocate is Jesus Christ, including his humility and service, which both was his glory and led to his glorification (Philippians 2:1-11).[19] Commitment to humble service and truthful speech, along with corresponding abdication of power and disdain for soothing ideologies, requires readiness to face failure and suffering, and, in some circumstances, even loss of life.[20]

To be morally grounded, public intellectuals require what Greeks have called *parrhesia*. It is freedom of speech, but not in the sense of the right of citizens to speak without hindrance (which, in Greek, is *isegoria*). *Parrhesia* is "candid speech and good counsel offered without fear or favor."[21] To affirm the good of open, truthful speech is implicitly to affirm the right of a person to just such open speech. The Acts of the Apostles, a text documenting the journey of the early followers of Christ from Jerusalem to imperial Rome, ends by stressing the importance of both *parrhesia* and *isegoria*. The very last

---

[18]On improvisation, see Miroslav Volf and Matthew Croasmun, *For the Life of the World: Theology That Makes a Difference* (Grand Rapids: Brazos, 2019), 107-14.

[19]See Volf and McAnnally-Linz, *Public Faith in Action*, 3-27.

[20]I apply here to Christian public intellectuals a passage from the New Testament (2 Timothy 4:3-5) about false teachers, who tailor their teaching to the desires of their listeners and therefore embrace myths, in contrast to true teachers, who are committed to truth and willing to endure suffering in its service.

[21]Peter Brown, *Power and Persuasion in Late Antiquity: Towards a Christian Empire* (Madison: University of Wisconsin Press, 1992), 65. Michel Foucault puts it this way: *parrhesia* "is a verbal activity in which a speaker expresses his personal relationship to truth, and risks his life because he recognizes truth-telling as a duty to improve or help other people (as well as himself)." See Foucault, *Fearless Speech*, ed. Joseph Pearson (Los Angeles: Semiotext(e), 2001), 19-20.

sentence has the apostle Paul "proclaiming the kingdom of God and teaching about the Lord Jesus Christ with all boldness [*parrhesia*]" and doing so "without hindrance" (Acts 28:31). Hindrances to free speech do not cancel the obligation to boldness, of course; they underscore the need for it.

Contribution. In the introduction, I noted three related but distinct tasks of public intellectuals. One is to help us understand the world in which we live. For centuries, the social world was relatively simple—"social world" designating here the world of economy, politics, technology, and communication, along with the impact of these on the environment; what we can describe, using Marxist idiom, as the combined effect of human *poiesis* and *praxis*. This simple world of yesteryear remained basically unchanged across wide spans of time: "What has been is what will be . . . nothing new under the sun" (Ecclesiastes 1:9). Today changes are far reaching and their pace breathtaking. The social world is exceedingly complex, with major transformations often happening under the surface, inaccessible to immediate observation. To identify and track the changes requires careful study. Public intellectuals do important work in helping the larger population understand the dynamics of change and its implications for human life.[22]

In a complex and fast-changing world, we also need help with identifying the best ways to achieve goals that concern the common good. The tools we must use to find our way in the world and make the world serviceable to our needs are understandably highly complex as well, tracking in complexity the social world in which they are put to use. The introduction of new materials and new

---

[22]For instance, to answer the question of whether climate change is the result of human activity or a natural occurrence within the ecosystem, we cannot rely on our immediate observation but must engage in scientific study of nature.

technologies has potential for both help and harm; some solutions are less costly than others, and so forth. If we are to adopt new technologies responsibly, we need public intellectuals to help us discern the effects of technologies on our individual lives, on communities, and on major institutions.

In the two tasks mentioned—understanding the world and designing and deploying technologies (which have to do, respectively, with explanatory and instrumental rationality)—the work of Christian public intellectuals will largely overlap with the work of public intellectuals of any other religious or secular orientation. Between these two tasks lies the third, which concerns human purposes.[23] At the heart of the Christian faith and Christian thinking about social issues is concern for the fundamental orientation in life, for the kind of life, individual and social, that is truly worthy of our humanity. This is not in the first instance a question of morality, about how we should behave, though moral questions are included in it; this is above all a question of human ontology, about who we are, about how we are set in the story of everything, and about the goal toward which we ought to stretch ourselves.[24]

To put the matter in the vocabulary of St. Augustine, Christian faith, and therefore Christian public engagement, is about what we should ultimately trust and what we should love above all things (and what we should, therefore, deeply mistrust and struggle against); it is about how we should live, as individuals, communities,

---

[23]This is where the specifically Christian contribution comes most into play. Christians have nothing unique to contribute to the question of what specific variations in the human genome are responsible for human intelligence; there are also no specifically Christian ways to design and deploy tools that would help us accomplish the task of "breeding" humans with superior intelligence. But there are Christian ways of deciding whether we should engage in this endeavor in the first place and, if we do, whether we should pursue eugenics at the embryonic stage.

[24]See Volf and Croasmun, *For the Life of the World*, 11-34.

and the entire human family, in the light of that trust and love. A Christian will answer all specifically moral questions—such as those about the legitimacy of eugenics, about whether we should make an effort to protect the bees and to what lengths we should go in doing so, about acceptable levels of difference in wealth across populations, or about the number of migrants who should be admitted to a country in a given year—all such questions a Christian should explore in the light of the answer to the question about what kind of life is worthy of our humanity.

Legitimacy. In the course of modernity, many became convinced that religion, believed to be an expression of unreason, should remain a strictly private affair; to make it public, especially in religiously pluralistic societies, would invite clashes across the lines of abiding differences and would leave us bereft of a shared way to adjudicate disputes. As a consequence, the idea of a Christian public intellectual became problematic. There should, perhaps, be public intellectuals who are Christians, the idea went, but there should not be any specifically Christian public intellectuals. Matters of common life ought to be decided on the basis of public reason, and convictions derived from positive revelation—from the Holy Scripture or the life and teaching of Jesus Christ—should not enter into deliberation.

The argument for the privatization of religion rests on the fiction of neutral, secular "public reason." Christians will resist it, and not just for their own sake but for the sake of the possibility of genuine common life with others, most of whom are adherents of some religion—as they will resist any form of religious intolerance. Nicholas Wolterstorff argues compellingly for an impartial political frame in which all persons have the right to equal voice as they participate in common life and the right to articulate their own positions in the way most aligned with their basic convictions.[25] Along with other public intellectuals, Christian public intellectuals are bearers of those same rights, though in exercising them they will have to pay careful attention to rhetorical situations, especially in pluralistic settings marked by tensions along lines of abiding differences and differentials in power.

Though the effectiveness of Christian public intellectuals is situationally dependent, their legitimacy is not. It rests in God's call to be improvisors of Christ and is an implicate of the love of neighbor—which is also love of the marginalized, the strangers, even love of the enemies. That kind of love is likely to involve both the *politics of embrace* and the *politics of agon*: willingness to create space in oneself for the other and, if invited, abide attentively in the space of the other, as well as readiness to engage with others in public contestation, an exercise that is categorically different from war, the goal of which is the destruction of the enemy.[26] Though *agon* has Nietzschean overtones and embrace has markedly Christic resonances, Jesus Christ in fact exemplifies both, and Christian public intellectuals will practice them guided by the example of Christ.

Modes of engagement. The way Christian public intellectuals will engage the wider public will depend on the concrete situation. Protestant Reformer Martin Luther was, arguably, a public intellectual. He lived and worked in a nondemocratic setting in which, with the exception of a Jewish minority (his treatment of whom is one of the

---

[25]Nicholas Wolterstorff, "The Role of Religion in Decision and Discussion of Political Issues," in *Religion in the Public Square: The Place of Religious Convictions in Political Debate*, by Robert Audi and Nicholas Wolterstorff (Lanham, MD: Rowman & Littlefield, 1997), 67-120. See also Jocelyn MacLure and Charles Taylor, *Secularism and Freedom of Conscience*, trans. Jane Marie Todd (Cambridge, MA: Harvard University Press, 2011).

[26]For rejection of war in favor of *agon* in Nietzsche, see Friedrich Nietzsche, "Homeric Contest," in *The Portable Nietzsche*, ed. Walter Kaufmann (New York: Viking, 1954), 32-39. For the appropriation of this distinction by a representative of agonistic democratic theory, see Chantal Mouffe, *The Democratic Paradox* (New York: Verso, 2000).

great stains on his legacy), all citizens were Christians. He addressed the rulers; he urged them to "fear God" and love their subjects, working tirelessly for their benefit; he also warned them that "a prince is a rare bird in heaven."[27] From the subjects he expected knowledge of what is right, but he insisted that they ought to submit even to exploitative and oppressive rulers, as during the 1524–1525 peasant rebellions, with unconscionable vehemence.[28] He saw no other way of avoiding chaotic forces from destroying the community.

Civil rights leader Martin Luther King Jr.—called Michael until his fifth birthday and then renamed in honor of the great Reformer who himself changed his family name from Luder to Luther, the "free one"—was also a Christian public intellectual.[29] He worked in a nation with strong democratic traditions and addressed the entirety of the population—citizens and their elected officials—by appealing to the basic convictions of the Christian faith, with which, in the middle of the last century, the great majority of US citizens strongly identified. He called for abolition of discriminatory racial laws and held the vision of a beloved community as the ideal for which to strive.

In the meantime, many erstwhile "Christian nations" have partly de-Christianized and become more pluralistic, both more secular and more multireligious. Christian public intellectuals will get a hearing and command respect to the degree that they are able to

---

[27]Martin Luther, "Magnificat," in *The Sermon on the Mount and the Magnificat*, Luther's Works 21 (St. Louis: Concordia, 1968), 357, 345. Also: God "did not permit any heathen king or prince throughout the length and breadth of the world to be praised, but, contrarywise, to be punished" (356).

[28]See the shift from a reasonably balanced text "Admonition to Peace: A Reply to the Twelve Articles of the Peasants in Swabia" (1525; in *Christian in Society III*, Luther's Works 46 [Philadelphia: Fortress, 1967], 17-43) and the subsequent brutal "Against the Robbing and Murdering Hordes of Peasants" (1525; in *Christian in Society III*, 49-55).

[29]On Martin Luther's change of his name, see Volker Leppin, *Martin Luther: A Late Medieval Life*, trans. Rhys Bezzant and Karen Roe (Grand Rapids: Baker Academic, 2017), 36-37.

address issues of common concern from a genuinely Christian perspective while highlighting convictions and using vocabulary with which non-Christians resonate. It may be that, in the future, Christian public intellectuals will work most effectively if they collaborate in ad hoc ways with people of different faiths and no faith at all but with shared specific concerns. Christian public intellectuals will also have to offer a vision of pluralistic political institutions that is true to Christian faith but acceptable to non-Christians on their own grounds.[30]

Finally, in many places today, however, Christians are struggling minorities living under regimes legitimized by ideologies hostile to the Christian faith. Often they are persecuted, and the "public" of Christian public intellectuals is reduced to their own self, their home, and the community of fellow believers. In the wider public, they will then appear as private citizens, not as public intellectuals. But even in such settings, many of those called to reflect on Christian faith—whether vocational or accidental theologians—will in fact *think and write* as public intellectuals. That is because the Christian faith has an inalienable public dimension; its concern is in fact God's relation to the entire world. Paul writing to the church in imperial Rome while in Corinth on a missionary journey or Paul writing to the church in Philippi while imprisoned in Rome was a pastoral and political theologian and therefore also a public intellectual, albeit a public intellectual whose reach was highly constrained.

Sphere of concern. When we think of public intellectuals today, we tend to think of them as addressing issues of common concern in a circumscribed social space: a city, a region, a nation. This is as it should be, because each community has its own specific set of

---

[30]For one such attempt, see Miroslav Volf, *Flourishing: Why We Need Religion in a Globalized World* (New Haven, CT: Yale University Press, 2016), 18-21, 97-137.

common concerns about its own shared life. Yet a Christian public intellectual can never lose from sight the world as a whole. Each community is not an isolated particular, but a concrete entity in Georg Friedrich Wilhelm Hegel's sense of "concrete" as a nodal point of complexly mediated interactions. More importantly, the planetary scope of care is for Christians given with the affirmation of God's unity: the one God is the God of the whole world. The Christian Bible in fact begins and ends with the entire world in view. At the beginning, the Garden of Eden, the original home of God, encompasses the entirety of existing humanity; at the end, the new Jerusalem, the home of God that was created at the end of human exile, is a single world encompassing the entire humanity.

Between the beginning and the end, there is a history of salvation: it begins with a single couple, Abraham and Sarah. From the start, they are called to go from their kindred and their parents' houses and given a promise that through them "all the families of the earth shall be blessed" (Genesis 12:3). Every Christian is an adopted child of Abraham and Sarah, called to leave the exclusive ties and primary allegiance to one's own native community and—united with Christ through the Spirit—love God above all things and be a blessing potentially to any person anywhere. Every Christian public intellectual is called to be just that kind of child of Abraham and Sarah. Common goods that are the matter of common concern are the goods of the world understood as God's home; they therefore encompass the entirety of the large and immensely diverse community of creation.

An important tradition, articulately represented by Plato, insisted that the moral shape of the larger community and of the souls of its members parallel each other.[31] In the New Testament, the idea is

---

[31]See Plato, *Republic* 441c-442d; see also Aristotle, *Politics* 1280b.

implicit in the conviction that the self, the church, and the world are—and are to become—God's dwelling place. To make the entire world, imagined as God's home, an object of care presupposes a capacious self and one that is most properly itself only as the unique and dynamic site of complexly mediated interactions and resonances with the entirety of that hoped-for divine home. To put the point in a theological rather than Hegelian idiom, it presupposes a catholic personality, a soul as an anticipatory microcosm of the reality to which the Seer in the book of Revelation points, exclaiming: "See, the home of God is among mortals" (Revelation 21:3). Fostering these kinds of selves, first of all in oneself and then also in others, is among the chief responsibilities of a Christian public intellectual.

2

The Spirit,
the Common Good,
and the Public Sphere

The Twenty-First-Century Public Intellectual
in Apostolic Perspective

Amos Yong

The intersection where theologians meet up with public intellectuals has waxed and waned over the past century. In this chapter, I revisit this crossroads from my own milieu as a Pentecostal and evangelical scholar whose more recent work has been in the arena of theological interpretation of Scripture. In the latter context, I have been asking, to put it crassly, What would the apostles do?[1]

---

[1]My book *The Hermeneutical Spirit: Theological Interpretation and the Scriptural Imagination for the 21st Century* (Eugene, OR: Cascade Books, 2017) takes up this conversation in dialogue predominantly with Luke–Acts, the latter of this ancient biblical author's two books being a narrative about the early Christian or apostolic experience. I develop what I call a pent-evangelical theological vision in Amos Yong, *The Future of Evangelical Theology: Soundings from the Asian American Diaspora* (Downers Grove, IL: IVP Academic, 2014). On the waning of the public intellectual, especially in the North American context, see Russell Jacoby, *The Last Intellectuals: American Culture in the Age of Academe* (New York: Basic Books, 2000); Richard A. Posner, *Public Intellectuals: A Study of Decline*, 2nd ed. (Cambridge, MA: Harvard University Press, 2003); the fortunes of the theologian attempting to work at this nexus have been affected within the arc of this broader decline (Posner's account).

Applied to the consideration of the work of the public intellectual, at least as historically manifest, the apostolic narrative invites reconceptualization of the assignment as one involving engagement with a plurality of publics in a variety of discursive activities, directed toward the coming divine reign. The following elaborates on this hypothesis in three steps (corresponding to the three sections of this essay): (1) assessing what may be perceived as a paradigmatic account of apostolic public speech, (2) presenting observations about the plurality of apostolic engagements with the variety of public squares encountered across imperial Rome and sketching their implications for contemporary public theologians embarking on the public intellectual vocation, and (3) culminating with an exploratory consideration of apostolic speech-acts and their implications for rethinking the theologian as public intellectual and as performer of public intellectual work in the present era. This essay is motivated by this question: If public intellectuals can be critics, scientists, or professionals, and even also theologians, what are the theological norms operative for public intellectual work?[2]

Before proceeding, I note that my thinking about the theologian as public intellectual builds on my prior work as a political and public theologian.[3] These are not identical dimensions of theological labor, but they can be and are related. My bringing these together may be suggestive also of ways in which the traditional understanding of the public intellectual might be theologically enriched. My objective is neither to reduce the theological character of public

---

[2]See John Michael, *Anxious Intellects: Academic Professionals, Public Intellectuals, and Enlightenment Values* (Durham, NC: Duke University Press, 2000), part 2.

[3]Political theology and public theology are not identical; my own thinking about the former, however, has been as part and parcel of the latter. See Amos Yong, *In the Days of Caesar: Pentecostalism and Political Theology—The Cadbury Lectures 2009*, Sacra Doctrina: Christian Theology for a Postmodern Age (Grand Rapids: Eerdmans, 2010).

intellectual work to a branch of political or public theology nor to say that all political or public theologians ought also to be public intellectuals. Rather, I propose that one way to revitalize theological discourse for public impact includes considerations developed within the subdisciplines of political and public theology. More precisely, and now linking back to this essay's broader thesis, the wager here is that my own political and public theology, encapsulated in the moniker "many tongues, many political practices," can also spark new imaginative possibilities for theological embrace of the public intellectual task.[4] This could help clarify how we might work together and in common, from our diverse locations. Rather than being directly persuasive about the common good—what some might take the telos of the modern public intellectual to be—the apostolic effort was focused on heralding the divine rule. Such a focus can be considered a complementary theological anticipation of the goal of public intellectual work.

"The Crowd Gathered": Pentecost as Public (Intellectual) Phenomenon

At the outset, let me hazard discussing the work of the public intellectual without attempting to define such, not only because I think its present forms are unpredictably malleable but also because I hope to venture an explicitly theological thesis, one that seeks to (re) inform the efforts of those aspiring toward such work by retrieving the apostolic testimony. In doing so, I risk being anachronistic: what the apostles were doing two thousand years ago can hardly be said to be like what the modern public intellectual essays. Yet I press on

---

[4]This is found in Yong, *In the Days of Caesar*; see also Amos Yong, "Many Tongues, Many Practices: Pentecost and Theology of Mission at 2010," in *Mission After Christendom: Emergent Themes in Contemporary Mission*, ed. Ogbu U. Kalu, Edmund Kee-Fook Chia, and Peter Vethanayagamony (Louisville: Westminster John Knox, 2010), 43-58, 160-63.

precisely because the fluidity of the phenomenon of public engagement invites normative consideration, which for theologians involves scriptural assessment at some level. Here, perhaps surprisingly, the ancient author known as St. Luke may prove more helpful than initially surmised.

Luke—here I go with the traditional consensus about the authorship of the Gospel of Luke and the Acts of the Apostles, on which argument for the thesis of this theological (rather than historical or exegetical) essay does not depend—was certainly not writing for the public in any contemporary sense of that notion. Yet it is well known that he situated his narrative in public space, in fact, in the widest of such spaces, that of imperial Rome. Clearly the first few chapters of the Third Gospel locate the narrative squarely in this public and political realm, when he identified these events as occurring "In the days of King Herod of Judea" (Luke 1:5); "In those days [when] a decree went out from Emperor Augustus that all the world should be registered" (Luke 2:1); and "In the fifteenth year of the reign of Emperor Tiberius, when Pontius Pilate was governor of Judea, and Herod was ruler of Galilee, and his brother Philip ruler of the region of Ituraea and Trachonitis, and Lysanias ruler of Abilene" (Luke 3:1).

If the entirety of the Jesus story for Luke unfolds on this political ground, his sequel, which explicitly builds on the first book (see Acts 1:1), brings the story to the farthest edges of the known world. "And so we came to Rome"—as one interpreter translates Acts 28:16—introduces the final scene of that book by situating the closing events at the heart of the Pax Romana itself.[5] The phrase communicates how Luke envisioned his story as encompassing the social and

---

[5]Paul W. Walaskay, "And So We Came to Rome": The Political Perspective of St Luke, Society for New Testament Studies Monograph Series 49 (Cambridge: Cambridge University Press, 1984).

political world as he and his contemporaries knew it. In short, if Luke is not a political or public theologian in any modern sense, and even if he can in no way be said to have been a public intellectual, he was equally as certainly recounting how the lives of Jesus (the Gospel) and his followers (Acts) were inevitably political and public vis-à-vis the circumstances of their own times.

Against this backdrop, I wish to attend more carefully to Luke's account of the day of Pentecost—after Jesus' ascension, the leading event framing the experiences of the earliest disciples. Of course, I do so in part because that has been the site of much of my work as a constructive Pentecostal theologian over the years—to which references will be provided in due course—but I now return (again) to this text, given my (re)discovery of its relevance for our topic. Note the geopolitical cues such as that which situates Luke's Pentecost narrative: that then and there "there were devout Jews from every nation under heaven living in Jerusalem" (Acts 2:5). In the following scenario, Luke intends to communicate that not only these Jews but also proselytes or Gentile converts to Judaism (Acts 2:10) came from across the known world. The list of sixteen nations (Acts 2:9-11) is shorthand for the ancient Hebraic lists of seventy nations, which are means of encompassing the whole human family.[6] Luke's cosmic horizon is unmistakable—thus he is concerned to stipulate clearly that the present time of his writing and of those who are reading his words is "the time of *universal restoration* that God announced long ago through his holy prophets" (Acts 3:21, italics added)—and it is just as clearly of political and public scope.

Yet Luke was not content merely to locate the day of Pentecost in this sociopolitical and public space; the characters he introduced

---

[6]See my essay, "'As the Spirit Gives Utterance . . .': Pentecost, Intra-Christian Ecumenism, and the Wider *Oekumene*," *International Review of Mission* 92, no. 366 (July 2003): 299-314.

also communicate with public intent. St. Peter, the leading spokesperson for the apostles, is presented as addressing those who were "from every nation under heaven": "Peter, standing with the eleven, raised his voice and addressed them, 'Men of Judea and all who live in Jerusalem, let this be known to you'" (Acts 2:14). To undergird his message authoritatively, Luke specifies that Peter drew from the prophetic tradition in this way: "This is what was spoken through the prophet Joel: 'In the last days it will be, God declares, that I will pour out my Spirit upon all flesh'" (Acts 2:16-17). To be doubly clear about Joel's prophecy (and Peter's intent), the "all flesh" is elaborated to include sons and daughters (who among the human family is not one or the other?) and young and old (any of us are younger or older), so that the all-inclusiveness of those on whom the Spirit is being poured out is undeniable.

The conclusion of the ancient prophet is also brought forth in addressing the known (Petrine and Lukan) world: "Then everyone who calls on the name of the Lord shall be saved" (Acts 2:21). Beyond that, Luke explicates that Peter himself drew his sermon to a close by saying that to those who repent and are baptized among the hearers (and readers of this text, by extrapolation): "the promise is for you, for your children, and for all who are far away, everyone whom the Lord our God calls to him" (Acts 2:39). If three thousand persons responded to Peter's Pentecost message (Acts 2:41), the possibility remains that any and all who might still hear this invitation can be (ongoing) recipients of this divine gift. Luke's description of what happens in the aftermath of this mass baptism leaves no doubt: "And day by day the Lord added to their number those who were being saved" (Acts 2:47).[7]

---

[7]My book *The Spirit Poured Out on All Flesh: Pentecostalism and the Possibility of Global Theology* (Grand Rapids: Baker Academic, 2005) is based not only on Acts 2:17 (from which the title derives) but also on the cosmic horizon of the Pentecost message.

I have two sets of comments, coming forward into our own time and addressing our present concerns. First, let us make explicit the connections between the universality of the Pentecost account and the broader-than-ecclesial dimensions of the contemporary public intellectual domain. Of course, we have always recognized Pentecost has a cosmic vista, but we have not usually comprehended such breadth of scope with the political and public spheres of life, surely not with the realm wherein and within public intellectuals trade. So, to be clear: Luke is not developing a theology of public intellectualism. However, his Pentecost vision—which is summarized in Acts 2 and provides the narrative arc for the entirety of the apostolic enterprise—includes the sociopolitical dimension and in that sense can be said to have public purchase, including, when brought forward into our late modern context, public intellectual implications. Put alternatively, Luke's Pentecost theology directed toward those "from every nation under heaven" may have more to tell us about a contemporary theology of public intellectual activity than we may have previously surmised.

Brought forward, then, Luke's apostolic narrative invites contemporary messianic disciples to embrace the public aspects of their faithful witness and then also urges Christians to explicate their theology of discipleship as involving public dimensions. In the twenty-first century, the age of transnational migration and internet, the local is also the global and vice versa. Christian witness in general and theological speech in particular are then also local and global concurrently, even if in different respects. To be thus local and global together prompts theological reflection and articulation to be attentive to the pluralism of their audiences, both intended and not. Just as the apostolic witness on the day of Pentecost was both particular and universal through many tongues and in multiple directions, so also contemporary Christian witness is and should be carried out. The apostolic speech was heard in many languages. In the third millennium, this involves simultaneous resounding across borders, cultures, and continents, whether through Google Translate or other media. Today's public intellectual already has a global audience, so theologians drawn to this charge will also need to do so globally.[8] As Peter spoke locally but with cosmic reach, so also today's theologians may write and speak to the church, but their words will be amplified, through digital and other means, globally.

Second, then, we might ask more about the normative character of such a Lukan political and even public theologian that might also be relevant to the public intellectual project and how such might be developed. Surely the cacophony of glossolalia prompted bewilderment, astonishment, and perplexity (Acts 2:6-7, 12), but also the crowd's recognition that "in our own languages we hear them speaking about God's deeds of power" (Acts 2:11). From this, the public invitation was to salvation in Jesus's name (Acts 2:21), effectively repentance, baptism in Jesus's name, forgiveness of sins, and reception of the Holy Spirit (Acts 2:38).

The immediate implications of such pneumatic inundation is the formation of the economic community of mutuality and reciprocity: the three thousand "had all things in common; they would sell their possessions and goods and distribute the proceeds to all, as any had need" (Acts 2:44-45).[9] It is clear that Luke does not have any contemporary notion of a common good in mind in telling of the Pentecost event. Instead, his account is about the outpouring of the divine wind, one that inaugurates the so-called last days, which are themselves much less the end times of speculative prophetic charts

---

[8]See Michael C. Desch, ed., *Public Intellectuals in the Global Arena: Professors or Pundits?* (Notre Dame, IN: University of Notre Dame Press, 2016).

[9]See my reading of Acts in this socioeconomic direction in Amos Yong, *Who Is the Holy Spirit?: A Walk with the Apostles* (Brewster, MA: Paraclete, 2011), part 2.

than the messianic reign of justice and shalom foretold by Israel's prophets, such as Joel. Yet the latter is surely—and by extension so is Peter's and Luke's Pentecost miracle—about the renewal of the human *polis* in all of its brokenness. So although Luke does not develop a Pentecost theology of the common good that syncs up nicely with our current understanding, he does present, through Peter in this specific case, a vision for human renewal, redemption, and well-being informed by the visitation of the divine wind.

But if Luke is not a political or economic theologian in our understanding of these terms, his Pentecost message was not merely idealistic or otherworldly. Instead, the coming of the divine wind had material consequences of the sort that anticipated the renewal and right-ordering of the common realm.[10] The implications for contemporary Christian faith are that its witness is inevitably public and political. Christian theological speech, by extension, also has a public and political character with performative and practical implications. Christian theologians may not be public intellectuals with any intentionality approximating the common understanding of the latter, yet their witness to the divine rule can and should herald a common and public goodness.[11]

"Listen to What I Have to Say!": Apostolic Speech as Public (Intellectual) Discursive Engagements

In this section, we look at two categories of apostolic speech given in public contexts: (1) among crowds in general and (2) to narrowly

---

[10]Arguably, the numinous or the mystical generates collective action and even activism. See, e.g., Walter Marschner, "Ritual and the Holy in Social Struggles: The Mysticism of Peasant Movements as a Challenge to Public Theology," in *Public Theology in Brazil: Social and Cultural Challenges*, ed. Eneida Jacobsen, Rudolf von Sinner, and Roberto E. Zwetsch, trans. Luís Marcos Sander and Hedy L. Hofmann, Theologie in der Öffentlichkeit [Theology in the Public Square] 6 (Berlin: LIT, 2013), 115-30.

[11]For more on Acts's missiology of Christian witness, see Amos Yong, *Mission After Pentecost: The Witness of the Spirit from Genesis to Revelation*, Mission in Global Community (Grand Rapids: Baker Academic, 2019), 171-80.

circumscribed audiences (of one, even). Building on the preceding discussion, I have two objectives for what follows. One is to canvass how the public character of the day of Pentecost phenomenon is disclosed pluralistically in the rest of the apostolic witness described in the book of Acts. The other is to draw out implications for our thinking about and engaging the public (intellectual) aspects of contemporary theologizing. We shall see that the many-tongues/nations aspect of the Pentecost narrative can be observed as carrying out the apostolic message in many public contexts and for various purposes related to the inauguration of divine reign. Therefore, contemporary (public) theologians are invited to address—and therefore have to be prepared or have to ready themselves to engage with—these multiple spheres and arenas in terms of the here-and-coming divine rule.

Apostolic exchanges with large groups. We cannot be exhaustive in our treatment, but apostolic exchanges with the masses might be grouped into two subcategories: (1) those that are noticeable for how they advance the Pentecost message and (2) those that provide more expansive perspective on apostolic strategies for engaging a pluralistic public sphere.[12] With regard to the former, observe first that the apostles, incarcerated for healing the man at the Beautiful Gate, are delivered from prison by an angel and instructed to "Go, stand in the temple and tell the people the whole message about this life" (Acts 5:20). While carrying out precisely this errand, they are questioned by the authorities. We find confirmation that this "whole message" concerns Jesus—his life, death, and exaltation, his offer of repentance and forgiveness of sins, and his gift of the Holy Spirit

---

[12]Darrell L. Bock, *A Theology of Luke and Acts: God's Promised Program, Realized for All Nations* (Grand Rapids: Zondervan, 2012), 336-40, rightly notes that the Lukan "crowds" function mainly as a foil in the book of Acts, as indicative of how the people accept or, mostly, reject the gospel. Nevertheless, I would maintain, our own theological reading of this narrative can appropriately seek to mine normative insights for contemporary public engagement.

(Acts 5:30-33)—consistent with that pronounced by Peter on the day of Pentecost.

Later, in the city of Samaria, Philip "proclaimed the Messiah" to the gathered crowds (Acts 8:5), including "the good news about the kingdom of God and the name of Jesus Christ" (Acts 8:12). Further, as relevant at this kerygmatic juncture of evangelistic proclamation, in Antioch in Pisidia, "almost the whole city gathered to hear" (Acts 13:44) Paul and Barnabas, where and when they announce clearly how the Jewish rejection of God's offer of eternal life means that this will now be made available to the Gentiles, "so that you may bring salvation to the ends of the earth" (Acts 13:47, here quoting from Isaiah 49:6).

A number of summary comments are here warranted. First, the apostolic witness in the public square is decidedly theological, concerning the good news of eternal life available in Jesus Christ. Second, however, this gospel is messianic, meaning related to the anointed representative that represents and inaugurates the divine plan to renew Israel, and hence the world to come is thereby interlaced with the present life in all its depth and density. Finally, this messianic renewal extends from Israel to the world of the Gentiles, so that divine salvation has universal and cosmic horizons.[13]

All of this reiterates what we have already seen in the Pentecost event, but here I wish to observe further their implications for contemporary public theological (and intellectual) work. The theologian as public intellectual ought to be no less than resolutely theological. Such explicitly theological talk risks marginalizing the public and intellectual relevance of that message in a contemporary pluralistic

---

[13]See, e.g., Paul S. Chung, *Public Theology in an Age of World Christianity: God's Mission as Word-Event* (New York: Palgrave Macmillan, 2010); Chung, *Hermeneutical Theology and the Imperative of Public Ethics: Confessing Christ in Post-colonial World Christianity* (Eugene, OR: Pickwick, 2013).

and secular world, so *how* such speech is conducted is as important as *what* is said.

We will return to this momentarily. Meanwhile, it is important to highlight that the soteriological content of theological speech concerns not just the spiritual or postmortem world to come but also includes this messianic dimension that seeks to renew the present order in anticipation of the impending divine reign. From this perspective, the public theologian (and intellectual) is invited to comprehend more thoroughly and expansively the complexities of contemporary political life in order to be able to take up the present opportunities and challenges more intentionally, strategically, and effectively.[14]

This is perhaps one reason why theologians today may be less inclined to the public intellectual vocation, simply because the lifetime taken to master one discursive field—theology in this case—impedes getting up to snuff on any other domain of inquiry, whether the political, the economic, the social, or the environmental. My point is not to condone theologians' speaking irresponsibly into these other spheres just because doing one's homework is so difficult, but to acknowledge that it takes time, patience, and laborious effort to gain the necessary knowledge and skills to navigate from the theological to substantive interface with these public domains. Many theologians may feel called indeed into the public intellectual arena, but invariably few prove themselves to be chosen.

The next subset of examples of public apostolic speech complicates further the pluralism of the common space but also provides cues for the theological vocation in a pluralistic world. Here what

---

[14]Vinoth Ramachandra, *Subverting Global Myths: Theology and the Public Issues Shaping Our World* (Downers Grove, IL: IVP Academic, 2008), e.g., attempts to take on public issues such as terrorism, religious violence, human rights, multiculturalism, science, and postcolonialism.

Luke describes as happening in Lystra, Athens, and Ephesus recites how apostolic speech intermingles with a plurality of religious and philosophical discourses. In Lystra, the healing of a man crippled from birth led the crowds to view Barnabas and Paul as manifestations of Zeus and Hermes (Acts 14:11-12), and this motivates them to bear witness to the city's inhabitants by deploying natural theological ideas about God as creator and sustainer of the world and its nations rather than delving more strictly into messianic or more Israel-centric themes.[15] We see similarly at the Areopagus that among Epicurean and Stoic interlocutors (Acts 17:18), Paul draws on the religious, poetic, and philosophic resources available within that broader Greco-Roman milieu (Acts 17:28) to present a more natural theological argument regarding the divine Creator, who makes himself known and available to the world, even if in this case Paul concludes with a direct allusion to the coming divine judgment mediated through God's resurrected agent (Acts 17:31).[16]

Finally, along these lines, at Ephesus, the home city of "the great goddess Artemis" (Acts 19:27), we see a businessman upset that Paul's (and his colleagues') preaching has dampened sales of the Greek deity's paraphernalia. Subsequently a raucous crowd (that includes some provincial officials) gathers at the theater and threatens harm when the town clerk calms them down by clarifying, among other things, that the accused Christians "are neither temple robbers nor blasphemers of our goddess" (Acts 19:37). The point to be made is a negative but important one: that whatever else has been understood

---

[15]See Marianne Fournier, *The Episode at Lystra: A Rhetorical and Semiotic Analysis of Acts 14:7-20a*, American University Studies 197 (New York: Peter Lang, 1997).

[16]Paul Copan and Kenneth D. Litwak, *The Gospel in the Marketplace of Ideas: Paul's Mars Hill Experience for Our Pluralistic World* (Downers Grove, IL: IVP Academic, 2014), is a bit more apologetic in approach; see also Clare K. Rothschild, *Paul in Athens: The Popular Religious Context of Acts 17*, Wissenschaftliche Untersuchungen zum Neuen Testament 341 (Tübingen: Mohr Siebeck, 2014).

as the content of Paul's message, his opposition to idolatry (see Acts 17:29) and preaching of the gospel does not include denigration, desacralization, or demonization of Artemis.[17]

What then are the implications for contemporary public (intellectual) theologizing? There is surely the rhetorical dimension that ought to be addressed, in particular recognizing local contexts (such as that of Ephesus, wherein Artemis predominates) within global flows. There is also what I might call the kerygmatic dimension: how to communicate theologically and respectfully in a pluralistic space. More substantively, public theologians hence need also to be comparative philosophers and comparative religionists in some respect, having knowledge about other wisdom and related traditions, so that their discursive articulations can operate in these common— and thereby pluralistic—environments, not so much to avoid offense (there will always be a scandalous dimension to the gospel) but because the intellectual undertaking involves thoughtful negotiation with the complexity of other persons, groups, and discourses.[18]

The public sphere is never politically, socially, or economically neutral, but these domains are always overlaid or sustained by values derived from underlying indigenous and local but also more global religious, philosophical, and wisdom traditions.[19] The work of the theologian as public intellectual thus invites sustained immersion— study, research, and experiential participation—in the intersecting worlds that constitute today's global public square.[20]

---

[17]My rephrasing of Craig S. Keener, *Acts: An Exegetical Commentary* (Grand Rapids: Baker Academic, 2014), 3:2937.

[18]For instance, Christian public intellectual discourse will need to encounter and interact with those emerging out of East Asian traditions; e.g., Tu Wei-Ming, *Way, Learning, and Politics: Essays on the Confucian Intellectual* (Albany: State University of New York Press, 1993).

[19]Miroslav Volf, *A Public Faith: How Followers of Christ Should Serve the Common Good* (Grand Rapids: Brazos, 2011), thus rightly urges Christians to embrace pluralism as political project.

[20]Thus my own motivation at the beginning of my theological vocation in the task of comparative theology, wherein my focus has been on Buddhist traditions; see, e.g., Amos Yong, *Pneumatology*

Apostolic exchanges to targeted audiences. My last set of comments in this section focuses on Luke's characterization of St. Paul's three extended apologies in the book of Acts, each of which are public albeit in different respects.[21] The first (Acts 22:1-21) occurs in some respects before "all the city" of Jerusalem (Acts 21:30), even if Paul addresses himself primarily to his Jewish compatriots from the temple steps (Acts 21:40). The next two are before governmental officials: Felix the governor of the province of Judea (Acts 24:10-21) and Herod Agrippa, a Roman client-king over Judea and its surrounding territories (Acts 26:2-29).

The former seeks mostly for self-absolution from charges against Paul brought by the Jewish authorities, without minimizing the theological aspect. This includes reference to his belief in the resurrection from the dead, which is underscored as being the source of agitation between him and his accusers. The latter, Herod, is much more intensely testimonial but includes a persuasive aspect, appealing that the king consider his own personal response to the witness of the good news of the Messiah sent for the world. Of course, these narratives constitute Luke's own apology for Christianity.[22] They also give us additional windows into the public nature of apostolic life and witness.

Personal testimony in this case can be public in at least two ways: commencing in public space or given before public officials, almost to an audience of one. Even in the latter instance, such witness has

---

and the Christian-Buddhist Dialogue: Does the Spirit Blow Through the Middle Way?, Studies in Systematic Theology 11 (Boston: Brill, 2012); Yong, The Cosmic Breath: Spirit and Nature in the Christianity-Buddhism-Science Trialogue, Philosophical Studies in Science & Religion 4 (Boston: Brill, 2012).

[21]I skip over Luke's portrayal of Paul before the high priest Ananias and the council of Sadducees and Pharisees (Luke 22:30–23:10) because this is much less of a public environment than the others I focus on here.

[22]See John W. Mauck, Paul on Trial: The Book of Acts as a Defense of Christianity (Nashville: Nelson Reference, 2001).

public implications and possibly effects, including the result that carves out public and private interests, such as that pronounced by Agrippa that the Pauline case does not belong in the realm of public or state adjudication (Acts 26:32).

What are some takeaways for public theologians then considering public intellectual work? First, the Acts account suggests that the testimony, while a profoundly personal matter, has the potential for public diffusion. If modernity separates the public from the religious or the common from the private, the apostolic narrative indicates that there are moments when these intersect. More important, the bearing of witness to the gospel, even for the public intellectual endeavor, cannot but be personal and testimonial in some respect. When and where this is called for or may be effective is an ongoing occasion for discernment.

Second, and just as relevant, public encounter involves knowing both one's audience, especially if these are governmental officials, and their contexts. The latter may be imbibed experientially and over time, but effective interaction with the public sphere gains from sound knowledge of historical and social dynamics and of legal and political currents. In today's climate, public theologians are made—oftentimes through prolonged research and study—not born; similarly, public intellectuals, even of the theological type, are forged through the anvil of inquiry rather than emerging overnight.[23] Putting these together means that an interesting tension emerges: on the one hand, public speech can be at its most affective when such comes from a deeply personal base; on the other hand, public relating includes the public other,

---

[23]It could be that theologians grow into a public intellectual vocation or gradually attain a public intellectual platform; Jürgen Moltmann, e.g., wrote two series of theological monographs before the appearance of his *God for a Secular Society: The Public Relevance of Theology*, trans. Margaret Kohl (Minneapolis: Fortress, 1999).

whether as individuals or groups, and hence the personal narrative will also have to effectually connect with these wider and broader realities.

"I Order You in the Name of Jesus Christ to Come Out of Her": Apostolic Speech-Acts in Public (Intellectual) Perspective

In this last section, I look at a specific type of apostolic interaction with the public sphere, namely, the apostles' speech-acts, and explore their ramifications for thinking about public theological work. The apostles do not merely speak publicly (we have already discussed some of their recorded addresses), but they also effect results with what they say, thus by definition turning speech into speech-acts. Such observations invite consideration of public theologizing in terms of not only what is verbalized but also what might be performed or achieved through such enunciations. This suggests the exploratory thesis that there is a performative dimension to public intellectual efforts, particularly when refracted through the apostolic lens.

Two examples in the book of Acts are worthy of note at this point. First, Stephen's apology is given to what seems to be a large group of people, including elders, scribes, and other witnesses (Acts 6:9-12; 7:58). But at the moment of his martyrdom, he prays, "Lord, do not hold this sin against them" (Acts 7:60). Thus Stephen's final public utterance is one of forgiveness, at least ensuring that his own conscience is freed from begrudging his enemies, but also declaring and thereby bringing about—implicitly in this scenario—their absolution from guilt.[24] Then, on the island of Malta, when Paul is hosted by "the leading man of the island, named Publius," it

---

[24]According to the Johannine Pentecost in which it was promised: "If you forgive the sins of any, they are forgiven them; if you retain the sins of any, they are retained" (John 20:23).

is said of the apostle that the only words he speaks are those of another form of prayer, in this case a petition for Publius's father, who "lay sick in bed with fever and dysentery," with the result that he is cured (Acts 28:7-8). In this case, even if privately uttered, the apostolic words have public effect, not only in that it is a public official's father who personally benefits but also in that such healing solidifies the apostolic standing with public opinion and effects the corresponding treatment. Apostolic words, hence, do not merely convey information, but they also shape public estimation and make social reality.

Another set of such speech-acts touches on that which we have introduced above, when the apostles were imprisoned by the oppositional Jewish leadership. In the early Christian community, such public speech was also an embodied form of what we would call civic disobedience. When challenged by the religious leadership and commanded to be silent, the apostolic response is, initially, "Whether it is right in God's sight to listen to you rather than to God, you must judge; for we cannot keep from speaking about what we have seen and heard" (Acts 4:19-20); and later, "We must obey God rather than any human authority" (Acts 5:29). These were words backed up with actions, or we could also say that they were words generated out of virtuous actions and commitments.[25] To the point, these speech-acts of resistance were born out of a stance protective of what we might today call religious freedom, but they might fit into the broader category of speaking truth to power, a familiar dynamic of public intellectual work, at least historically.[26]

---

[25]The voice of the public theologian resounds from out of a virtuously formed life that is in turn shaped liturgically by the gospel. So argues James K. A. Smith, *Awaiting the King: Reforming Public Theology* (Grand Rapids: Baker Academic, 2017).

[26]On this theme, see the essays in Amatai Etzioni and Alyssa Bowditch, eds., *Public Intellectuals: An Endangered Species?* (Lanham, MD: Rowman & Littlefield, 2006), part 6.

In response, before the same religious council, Gamaliel, a respected teacher, also speaks, concluding that "if it is of God, you will not be able to overthrow them—in that case you may even be found fighting against God!" (Acts 5:39).[27] Here, Gamaliel does not merely provide information, but he does something with his words; specifically, he warns his hearers. Thus apostolic sayings were also public actions of civic resistance even as Gamaliel's words were also a performative act of admonishment.

Perhaps the most unexpected observation in this regard concerns three instances of exorcism in the book of Acts that take place in public space. Luke tells us that the Samarian "crowds with one accord listened eagerly to what was said by Philip, hearing and seeing the signs that he did, for unclean spirits, crying with loud shrieks, came out of many who were possessed" (Acts 8:6-7). Thus we know that Philip is not only proclaiming about the Messiah and the coming rule of God (see also the discussion above) but also commanding unclean spirits to depart from their hosts.

Then, on the island of Cyprus, Paul and Barnabas are interrelating with the proconsul but interrupted by Elymas the magician; in this context, Luke details precisely not only the exorcistic utterance but also the aftermath, which occurs exactly as commanded, resulting in the proconsul's belief (Acts 13:10-12).

The final occasion then concerns the slave girl with a spirit of divination at Philippi, who attempts to make a spectacle of Paul and his colleagues. In that public space, Paul finally confronts the situation: "I order you in the name of Jesus Christ to come out of her";

---

[27]These apostolic stances against the religious status quo (that historically have since been co-opted by the wider public) anticipate what Sondra Farganis calls "dissenting intellectuals" who are self-critical also about their own social and intellectual location. See her essay, "A Public or Dissenting Intellectual?," in *The Changing Role of the Public Intellectual*, ed. Dolan Cummings (New York: Routledge, 2005), 157-71.

this directive results in a transformed situation that Luke simply describes thus: "And it came out that very hour" (Acts 16:18).

Although the Lukan point for these exorcisms has to do more with validating the apostolic ministry (of Philip and Paul in these cases), our own lenses highlight the very public nature of these acts of deliverance.[28] Apostolic public discourses include performative elements—in these cases, the casting out of unclean spirits and liberation of those held by such.

I sense that when colleagues consider the public intellectual duty, they pay little attention to the performative dimensions of such speech, beyond the rhetorical aspects designed to move the various publics being addressed in the directions commended by the speaker. But observing that apostolic public expression includes speech-acts that attempt to achieve various objectives, such as forgive or caution audiences, heal and deliver bodies in the public sphere, and resist the operative powers of the public square—all of this indicates that there is or can be a performative element to public intellectual work. Yes, public intellectual discourse attempts to influence and convince, but perhaps can also renew the common realm. It may be that there is an activist component to the public intellectual enterprise, one that not only persuades audiences but also enacts reality.[29]

If modern (Enlightenment) models of the public intellectual emphasized the cerebral character of rhetorical and persuasive argumentation, late modern transformations of this ideal type have insisted that the cognitive is interwoven with the affective and the

---

[28]Todd Klutz, *The Exorcism Stories in Luke-Acts: A Sociostylistic Reading*, Society for New Testament Studies Monograph Series 129 (Cambridge: Cambridge University Press, 2004), treats only the slave-girl narrative (plus three exorcisms in the Third Gospel), but his overarching assessment applies also to the other two texts I discuss here.

[29]See Ada María Isasi-Díaz, Mary McClintock Fulkerson, and Rosemary P. Carbine, eds., *Theological Perspectives for Life, Liberty, and the Pursuit of Happiness: Public Intellectuals for the Twenty-First Century* (New York: Palgrave Macmillan, 2013), xiv.

embodied—and thus the performative—and vice versa; whereas the intellectual and the activist were formerly of distinct, and even contrary, sorts, they are now understood as also being fused together.[30] The Lukan narrative indicates apostolic speech and activities were distinct but inevitably interwoven aspects of the one call to bear witness in the power of the Holy Spirit.

Public theologians in the present time surely ought to be discursively articulate, but they may and perhaps should be, as led by the Spirit of Pentecost, also practically engaged. Such apostolic insights would then urge that public theological and intellectual work not only formulates an abstract vision for the common good but also seeks to socially, materially, and concretely actualize such in our midst.

---

[30]The contrast in this way between modern and late modern models is evident not least when we consult public theological projects such as Dwight N. Hopkins, ed., *Black Faith and Public Talk: Critical Essays on James H. Cone's Black Theology and Black Power* (Waco, TX: Baylor University Press, 2007).

Part 2

Professional Reflections

3

Cultivating Public Intellectuals for the Common Good

Linda A. Livingstone

Public intellectuals play an important role in our society: they help people engage with important (and often difficult) ideas. For individuals who otherwise would not have the time, inclination, or resources to seek this knowledge out for themselves, this service is significant.[1] Public intellectuals also help political leaders, economic leaders, and other policymakers understand the far-reaching consequences of policies that may otherwise seem limited in scope.[2] Although public intellectuals have always existed in some form or another, for the past several centuries they have been strongly linked to the university system.[3] If you think of the intellectuals invited to comment on television or write op-eds in newspapers today, they tend to have terminal degrees. Many of them work at universities—or for institutes housed within universities. Intellectuals without such credentials are rare enough to be the exception that proves the rule.

---

[1] Edward Shils, "The Intellectuals and the Powers: Some Perspectives for Comparative Analysis," *Comparative Studies in Society and History* 1, no. 1 (1958): 5-22.

[2] Robert Presthus, *Men at the Top: A Study in Community Power* (New York: Oxford University Press, 1964).

[3] Randall Collins, "Why the Social Sciences Won't Become High-Consensus, Rapid-Discovery Science," *Sociological Forum* 9, no. 2 (June 1994): 155-77, www.jstor.org/stable/685040.

This connection between the university system and the broader world of intellect means university presidents need to ask ourselves several important questions about our roles as administrators and as intellectuals. What are our main responsibilities as university presidents? Should we be public intellectuals ourselves? What role, if any, do we play in developing or encouraging public intellectuals at our institutions? These questions are especially important for presidents of Christian universities as we seek to carry out our institutional missions.

The Historic University President in the United States

The first European universities, such as the University of Bologna, were havens where scholars supported one another within a context of academic freedom. It is not surprising, then, that a large part of a university chancellor's or president's responsibility has remained facilitating academic pursuits. As William Harper, founder and first president of the University of Chicago, puts it, "How does the president of a university spend his time? Largely in seeking ways and means to enable this or that professor to carry out some plan which he has deeply at heart."[4] What has changed, however, is the nature of those pursuits.

In the 1700s, the Enlightenment and the rise of utilitarian thinking spurred an explosion of interest in university education.[5] The emphasis on individual rationality embodied by these movements placed a premium on basic training in a variety of technical subjects that universities were best able to provide. The purpose of this training was to facilitate participation in the political and civic spheres.[6]

---

[4]William Harper, quoted in Harold Shapiro, "University Presidents: Then and Now" (speech, Princeton Conference on Higher Education, Princeton, NJ, March 1996), https://pr.princeton.edu/hts/speeches/9603-thennow.html.

[5]Collins, "Why the Social Sciences"; James D. Hunter and Paul Nedelisky, *Science and the Good: The Tragic Quest for the Foundations of Morality* (New Haven, CT: Yale University Press, 2018).

[6]John Brubacher and Willis Rudy, *Higher Education in Transition: History of American Colleges and Universities* (New York: Harper & Row, 1996); Mark C. Carnes, *Minds on Fire:*

It should not surprise us, then, that the politically minded founding fathers of the United States were deeply involved in higher education. Thomas Jefferson and James Madison were rectors at the University of Virginia, and before serving as the first president of the United States, George Washington served as chancellor at William & Mary. All three advocated for the establishment of federal universities. In his eighth annual message to Congress, the precursor to the modern State of the Union Address, George Washington stated:

> The primary object of such a national institution should be the education of our youth in the science of government. In a republic what species of knowledge can be equally important and what duty more pressing on its legislature than to patronize a plan for communicating it to those who are to be the future guardians of the liberties of the country?[7]

Here we see that the modern debate about public intellectuals would have been nonsensical at the time. The debate then was not whether academics should operate in civic and political spheres, but rather about their obligation to enrich civic and political life through engagement outside academia and through the training of the next generation of citizens and politicians. James Madison clearly tied higher education to the common good when he stated, "A popular Government, without popular information, or the means of acquiring it, is but a Prologue to a Farce or a Tragedy."[8]

How Role-Immersion Games Transform College (New Haven, CT: Yale University Press, 2014).

[7]George Washington, "Eighth Annual Message of George Washington," Washington, DC, December 7, 1796, https://avalon.law.yale.edu/18th_century/washs08.asp.

[8]James Madison to W. T. Barry, August 4, 1822, in *The Writings of James Madison*, ed. Gaillard Hunt (New York: G. P. Putnam's Sons, 1900), http://press-pubs.uchicago.edu/founders/documents /v1ch18s35.html.

This emphasis paints a picture of the ideal university president as both a disciplinarian and a spiritual counselor for students, a picture borne out by the history of early American colleges. American colleges developed from serving mostly as seminaries, and at the time of the Civil War, 91 percent of college presidents were still clergy.[9] Although American universities did not have the explicit religious tests of Oxford and Cambridge, college presidents considered the moral qualifications of their potential students when evaluating them for admission.[10] This is not to say that early college presidents did not work with boards of trustees or perform administrative tasks, only that they were primarily thought of as shepherds and role models.

The Industrial Revolution and the Shift in Higher Education

The role of higher education shifted over the 1800s as the Industrial Revolution made its way from Britain to the Americas. Technological advancement meant that technical skills were in high demand, which in turn led to a greater demand for institutions designed to impart those skills instead of the broader liberal-arts education favored even a few decades earlier.[11] At the same time, science was becoming a profession unto itself, evolving—from a hobby indulged in or sponsored directly by elite patrons—into a career.[12]

This period also saw an increased number of state schools and the creation of land-grant institutions. The Morrill Act of 1862 granted thirty thousand acres of federal land to states under the condition

---

[9]E. Brooks Holifield, *God's Ambassadors: A History of the Christian Clergy in America* (Grand Rapids: Eerdmans, 2007), 119.

[10]Brubacher and Rudy, *Higher Education in Transition.*

[11]Brubacher and Rudy, *Higher Education in Transition*; Collins, "Why the Social Sciences."

[12]George H. Daniels, "The Process of Professionalization in American Science: The Emergent Period, 1820–1860," *Isis* 58, no. 2 (Summer 1967): 150-66, https://doi.org/10.1086/350216.

that the proceeds be used to fund a college specifically intended to "teach such branches of learning as are related to agriculture and the mechanic arts . . . in order to promote the liberal and practical education of the industrial classes in the several pursuits and professions in life."[13] This put pressure on existing private colleges to tweak their curricula and emphasize science, which often came at the expense of the classical works that had dominated a few short decades before. Similarly, modern institutions are under pressure to bring this process to its conclusion and focus solely on skills that "prepare students for careers" over the humanities and the other liberal arts.[14]

As the number of students increased, universities developed bureaucracies. As these bureaucracies became more complex, university presidents were expected to become conversant in finance, law, and real estate, among their other duties. And as university presidents sought to become Renaissance men for their roles (and yes, they were mostly men), it became clear that administrating a university demanded a president's undivided attention. This marked the beginning of a transition among administrators: administration becoming the primary duty of presidents and chancellors, as opposed to one duty among many faculty members.[15]

By the 1900s, the supervision and teaching of students had been spun off into discrete functions within the bureaucracy, and college presidents began to function more like CEOs. As corporate entities,

---

[13]Morrill Act of July 2, 1862, Pub. L. No. 130, 12 Stat. 503 (1862).

[14]Audrey Collin and A. G. Watts, "The Death and Transfiguration of Career—and of Career Guidance?," *British Journal of Guidance & Counselling* 24, no. 3 (1966): 385-98, https://doi.org /10.1080/03069889608253023.

[15]Paul J. DiMaggio and Walter W. Powell, "The Iron Cage Revisited: Institutional Isomorphism and Collective Rationality in Organizational Fields," *American Sociological Review* 48, no. 2 (April 1983): 147-60, https://doi.org/10.2307/2095101; M. W. Meyer and M. C. Brown, "The Process of Bureaucratization," *American Journal of Sociology* 83, no. 2 (1977): 364-85; Max Weber, "Bureaucracy," in *Economy and Society*, ed. Guenther Roth and Claus Wittich (Berkeley: University of California Press, 1968), 956-1005.

institutions of higher learning need someone to manage multimillion-dollar budgets; navigate local, state, and federal legislative issues; and oversee hundreds or thousands of faculty and staff, all while ensuring that tens of thousands of students receive a competitive education.

It should be no wonder, then, that 40 percent of current university/college presidents are not academics, having never held a tenured or tenure-track position at any institution of higher learning.[16] The majority are academics, which suggests that there is still some legitimacy in having a working understanding of higher education from the inside. But experience in academia is starting to matter less than corporate acumen. It has become common for presidents to leave educational leadership strictly in the hands of provosts.

Presidents as Public Intellectuals

With this understanding of the role of presidents in both historic and contemporary colleges, we can more fully engage with the question of public intellectuals working for the common good, beginning with the role of presidents *as* public intellectuals.

As mentioned earlier, this discussion would be nonsensical in the historical context, because university presidents were almost all public intellectuals. As members of the clergy, they preached both to their student bodies and to their own churches, and many either had held public office or were elected after leaving their positions at the university. During the founding years of many colleges, the president was the only teacher, as was the case for James Manning at the College of Rhode Island.[17]

---

[16]Tressie M. Cottom, Sally Hunnicutt, and Jennifer A. Johnson, "The Ties That Corporatize: A Social Network Analysis of University Presidents as Vectors of Higher Education Corporatization," *SocArXiv*, May 22, 2018, https://doi.org/10.31235/osf.io/wpcfq.

[17]Richard G. Durnin, "The Role of the Presidents in the American Colleges of the Colonial Period," *History of Education Quarterly* 1, no. 2 (1961): 23-31.

However, we live in the contemporary era, where many colleges and universities have shifted their focus from the common good to *financialization*.[18] The most significant impact has been a long-sustained theme of American higher education: the drift toward secularism. A combination of both historical and social factors perpetuated this drift. Unlike private colleges, public colleges were not explicitly religious; in the mid-1800s, the public university began to be the norm.[19] The rise of accreditation and institutional pressures to replicate the success of public universities also led to increased secularization in higher education.[20] Secularization does not exclude charitable work or work for the public good, but lay presidents do not have the same structural impetus to spread the good word that clergy did with their congregations.

The corporate shift in the office of president discourages intellectual pursuits in general, and it certainly does not incentivize presidents to translate their scholarly pursuits into common parlance. As mentioned above, it is becoming common for modern college presidents not to be academics. This is the tradeoff of specialization and bureaucratization. The university president limits personal engagement in intellectual matters so that faculty do not have to engage as much in administration.

Finally, modern college presidents are heavily involved in fundraising, unlike historical presidents. At the institution I lead, one of my main responsibilities is to build relationships with donors and travel around the country to meet with alumni and friends of the university. The donors with whom I meet have a variety of views on the sorts of big questions with which public intellectuals

---

[18]Cottom, Hunnicutt, and Johnson, "Ties That Corporatize."
[19]Brubacher and Rudy, *Higher Education in Transition.*
[20]DiMaggio and Powell, "Iron Cage Revisited."

concern themselves, and most of our donors are working within the Protestant theological and philosophical tradition. I imagine there is an even greater variety of perspective among donors to secular institutions.

Whether university presidents are academics themselves or are among the 40 percent of presidents who come from nontraditional backgrounds, they should certainly support the development of public intellectuals on their campuses and in society at large. And they must be willing to stand for what they believe in. But as the leaders of our universities, we also have an obligation to balance our stance taking with our duty to protect and empower academic freedom for the professors who work at our universities. There are issues that are worth championing, and others that will unnecessarily alienate donors, prospective students, and governmental officials. Every university president has likely received phone calls about speakers being allowed on campus. During the Vietnam War protests across campuses in the 1960s, one of my predecessors at Baylor, as legend tells it, posted fliers across campus when he heard rumors of a war protest. He made it clear that any student who showed up to protest would be expelled and any faculty or staff member who showed up would be terminated. In today's higher-education landscape, those types of actions are unthinkable. Besides the general media outcry, neither faculty nor students would accept such dictates.

When a president speaks, she is perceived as speaking for her entire university. Because of this, we have a professional obligation to support the official mission of the institutions we represent. When we are rooted in those missions and the values that accompany them, we should speak from a position of strength. Lee Bollinger, president of Columbia University, has done important work fighting for affirmative action.[21] West Virginia University President Gordon Gee is working with John Kasich to help fight the opioid crisis afflicting many West Virginians.[22]

Furthermore, we live in a time when the value and importance of a college education is under attack.[23] As university presidents, we are well-positioned to advocate for higher education as a common good. But even when university presidents speak out on matters close to education, it does not always translate to legislation. For issues beyond our university's mission and values, even important social issues or the political scandal du jour, having our perspective be heard is less important than our obligation to protect the university and the scholars researching there.

Facilitating Public Intellectuals

Currently presidents are less likely than previously to influence the students at their colleges by lecturing, preaching, and administering discipline to individual students or even small groups.[24] This does not mean that university presidents cannot get involved in cultivating public intellectuals focused on the common good. I offer three ways university presidents *can* and *ought to* cultivate public intellectuals focused on the common good: encouraging research that addresses pressing issues, setting an example in leadership, and championing campus programs that build character in and transform the lives of students.

[21]Lee Bollinger, "What Once Was Lost Must Now Be Found: Rediscovering an Affirmative Action Jurisprudence Informed by the Reality of Race in America," *Harvard Law Review* 129 (April 12, 2016), https://harvardlawreview.org/2016/04/what-once-was-lost-must-now-be -found-rediscovering-an-affirmative-action-jurisprudence-informed-by-the-reality-of -race-in-america.

[22]John Kasich and E. Gordon Gee, "Don't Forget Our Frontline Caregivers in the Opioid Epidemic," *New York Times*, September 17, 2019, www.nytimes.com/2019/09/17/opinion/opioid -settlement-hospitals.html.

[23]Colleen J. Shogan, "Anti-Intellectualism in the Modern Presidency: A Republican Populism," *Perspectives on Politics* 5, no. 2 (2007): 295-303, https://doi.org/10.1017/S153759270707079X.

[24]Brubacher and Rudy, *Higher Education in Transition*.

Encouraging research that addresses pressing issues. Presidents have the ability to set policy that encourages research on pressing issues and builds character among the student body. For example, the chancellor of Rutgers University-Newark, Nancy Cantor, calls this "public scholarship."[25] One of the simplest ways to encourage this public scholarship is to honor the professors who go through media training and work with local, national, and international news stations to make high-level research accessible and comprehensible to everyday Americans. I want to highlight two such professors at Baylor—Byron Johnson and Bryan Brooks.

In 2012, the codirector for Baylor's Institute for the Studies of Religion, Byron Johnson, published a study that found that a faith-based prisoner reentry program reduced recidivism among Minnesota prisoners. The researchers estimated that the program saved an estimated $3 million by reducing rearrest, reconviction, and reimprisonment. Johnson said of the study, "This kind of research will be called for by policymakers. . . . Taxpayers want to know whether programs work—especially when religion is involved."[26]

In March 2019, one of our faculty members in environmental science, Bryan Brooks, received pharmaceutical company Recipharm's 2018 International Environmental Award for his research on environmental sustainability. Brooks discovered pharmaceuticals in the fish of certain Texas lakes, which explained several massive fish deaths. He now works internationally on designing chemicals that do not have the environmental hazards that could taint water quality and harm populations of animals and plants living in water.

---

[25]Nancy Cantor, "Taking Public Scholarship Seriously" (presentation, Syracuse University, Syracuse, NY, June 9, 2006).

[26]Byron Johnson, "Counting the Cost," *Baylor Magazine* (Fall 2013), www.baylor.edu/alumni/magazine/1201/news.php?action=story&story=133510.

At a recent meeting of Baylor's Council of Deans, Chris Rios, associate dean of Baylor's Graduate School, said, "Higher education rightly gets criticized for being terribly esoteric. A Christian university should be marked by its desires to promote human flourishing by sharing its distinct resources and abilities to further the common good."[27] It is incumbent on university presidents to encourage and celebrate research that furthers the common good.

Setting an example in leadership. The second way university presidents can cultivate public intellectuals who focus on the common good is to make concerted, strategic efforts to showcase their research, faith, and character. To begin my weekly President's Council meetings, one of our vice presidents offers a devotional and a prayer. Baylor also hosts conferences annually that link our faith mission to the pressing issues of the world. For example, Baylor's Institute for Faith and Learning hosts an annual Symposium on Faith and Culture, a three-day scholarly event addressing significant issues from the vantage point of Christian intellectual traditions. Previous themes have included Technology and Human Flourishing, Bottom-Up Approaches to Global Poverty, and the Character of the University.

When I began as Baylor's president, one of the top priorities was to chart a path to becoming a preeminent Christian research university by achieving R1 status, a designation given by the Carnegie Classification of Institutions of Higher Education that is reserved for American universities that engage in the highest levels of research activity. To achieve this goal, we developed an academic strategic plan called Illuminate, which calls Baylor to develop our research enterprise so that we can have influence in the public square. Our

---

[27]Chris Rios, "What Does It Mean to Be a Christian Research University?" (presentation, Lakeway Resort and Spa, Lakeway, TX, August 13, 2019).

team made maintaining an "unambiguously Christian educational environment" the first pillar of Illuminate.

I believe that if we want to point the scholarly community toward the public good, we have to do high-quality research and establish credibility. Then our Christian perspective can be heard. I believe that we must establish our credibility as legitimate among scholars if we want to have influence in the public square.

Ultimately, we seek to educate men and women for worldwide leadership and service by integrating academic excellence and Christian commitment within a caring community. As we have more influence as a university, we can graduate more doctoral students and conduct more meaningful research, which enables us to have more impact.

Championing transformational campus programs. The final way we can cultivate public intellectuals focused on the common good is to create campus programs that build character in and transform the lives of our students. Fortunately, higher education places a premium on building character in our students. Most universities offer programs that do not merely encourage civic and political engagement but also provide real, meaningful opportunities to engage. While there is a tendency to dismiss clubs and other student organizations as unimportant, campus organizations offer environments for students to learn leadership, time management, advocacy, and excellence in their work.[28] These opportunities for engaged learning help students develop a sense of purpose and link their education to practical skills.[29]

Some programs even enable students to engage directly with state or national politics. Because of universities' alumni networks,

---

[28]Carnes, *Minds on Fire.*

[29]F. D. Foubert and L. U. Grainger, "Effects of Involvement in Clubs and Organization on the Psychosocial Development of First-Year and Senior College Students," *NASPA Journal* 43, no. 1 (2006): 166-82.

program participants can often secure internships in legislative bodies, courthouses, and executive offices. These internships are not only organized and facilitated by the university but are also incentivized with course credit and linked with classes that focus on developing civic engagement in our students.

One of my predecessors, in conjunction with the then–student body president, formed the Baylor Ambassadors program, in which students travel to the Texas capitol to lobby for the Tuition Equalization Grant, which provides funds to help low-income and first-generation students afford private higher education in Texas, and the US capitol to lobby for federal legislation important to higher education. Another program, the Bob Bullock Scholars program, moves students to Austin for one semester and to intern full time during sessions of the Texas legislature. In another program, Semester in Washington, students earn six hours of course credit by interning nearly full time in Washington, DC, in the field of their choice.

It is also important that universities acknowledge and make space for discussion on hot-button topics. In his inaugural address as president of Harvard University, Lawrence Bacow noted,

> It is our responsibility to educate students to be discerning consumers of news and arguments, and to become sources of truth and wisdom themselves. . . . As faculty, it is up to us to challenge our students by offering them a steady diet of new ideas to expand their own thinking—and by helping them appreciate that they can gain much from listening to others, especially those with whom they disagree.[30]

---

[30]Lawrence Bacow, "Installation Address by Lawrence S. Bacow" (speech, Harvard University, Cambridge, MA, October 5, 2018), www.harvard.edu/president/speech/2018/installation-address -by-lawrence-s-bacow.

This sort of work demonstrates the role of university presidents in cultivating a love for the common good in our student bodies. In this way, we can sow seeds of character building in the tens of thousands of students who pass through our campuses.

For the 2019–2020 academic year, Baylor launched a university-wide initiative on civil discourse. It began with a faculty panel composed of Baylor professors from history, political science, English, and communication. Professors talked about humbling oneself before others, considering the context of offered opinions, and rejecting the "us versus them" mentality that pervades so much of our national discourse today. In another event, two professors from Biola University spoke on the art of winsome persuasion and how to exhibit Christian influence in a post-Christian world. To conclude the fall 2019 semester, Cornel West and Robert George visited our campus to model civil discourse between two scholars on different sides of the political spectrum (and who disagree on almost everything!).

The Christian Perspective

The structure of the university has changed considerably over the past two hundred years, and the administrative duties of a president eclipse many of their other responsibilities. But university presidents *can* and *ought to* cultivate public intellectuals focused on the common good by encouraging research that addresses pressing issues, setting an example in leadership, and championing campus programs that build character in and transform the lives of students. This task is not easy. But we have an obligation to complete it, and the end results are stronger universities, better people, and a stronger national/international community.

For Christians, there is a divine mandate that extends back to Genesis to steward the earth we have been given. We must be agents of change—in the world, but not of the world—in a society that needs the message of the gospel. For this reason, it is imperative that intellectuals and academics (and those of us who oversee them) engage not only with issues on our own campuses but also with the pressing issues facing our society, our nation, and our world.

4

Loving God and Neighbor

Heather Templeton Dill

Do not be afraid of pluralism. It is good for you.

PETER BERGER, "FAITH IN A PLURALIST AGE"

The reality of the twenty-first century is that religion has not gone away, as the happy advocates of the secularization theory had hoped. Rather, the dynamics of religious belief and practice are changing. Consider some of the findings from surveys conducted by the Pew Research Center and cofunded by the John Templeton Foundation. Although Christians (who include Catholics, Protestants, and Orthodox) outnumber all other faith traditions worldwide, Pew's research suggests that the global Muslim population will equal the global Christian population by 2050. Muslims will also become the largest minority faith in the United States, and the numbers of Buddhists, Hindus, and other religions living and practicing in the United States will double in size.[1] The rest of the world will likely

---

[1] Pew Research Center, "The Future of World Religions: Population Growth Projections, 2010–2050: Why Muslims Are Rising Fastest and the Unaffiliated Are Shrinking as a Share of the World's Population," April 2, 2015, https://assets.pewresearch.org/wp-content/uploads/sites/11/2015/03/PF_15.04.02_ProjectionsFullReport.pdf.

experience a similar melding of religious traditions. How then shall we live?

This question represents another opportunity for scholars to lend their voices to the conversation. Since 9/11, philanthropists and private foundations have focused more attention on the implications of a world where religious adherents of different faith traditions live in closer proximity to one another. Nonprofit leaders have also invested philanthropic resources to build bridges between religious groups. Eboo Patel started the Interfaith Youth Core in 2002 to encourage interfaith understanding and friendship among young people with the hope that future generations will appreciate what Rabbi Lord Jonathan Sacks has called the "dignity of difference." In 2012 the Aspen Institute created the Inclusive America Project to think about American democracy in the face of increasing religious and ethnic diversity in the United States. And in 2014 Pastor Bob Roberts and Imam Mohamed Magid established My Neighbor's Keeper to demonstrate that people from different faith traditions can live in peace when they unite around common causes or commitments.

Philanthropy has always tried to define the common good through their grant-making activities and other kinds of public advocacy. All of these efforts, however, must be rooted in a clear theoretical framework, a robust theology, or a thorough understanding of human psychology and sociology, to name just a few disciplines. This is where scholars, thought leaders, and public intellectuals come into the picture. A vision of the common good in the twenty-first century must recognize that religious pluralism is a defining feature of our life together. To be sure, the American experiment was predicated on freedom of conscience, and we have long valued the presence of multiple and diverse religious groups in the United

States. But these ideals sprung from a common religious heritage rooted in the Judeo-Christian tradition and, insofar as that common heritage unites fewer people in the United States and also around the world, it is time for Christians, in particular, to cultivate a way of thinking about interfaith relationships and the role and practice of the Christian faith in what Miroslav Volf has called "our ineradicably pluralistic world."[2]

There are two ways to do this. On the one hand, the development or rearticulation of theoretical constructs and new ideas and concepts can help us reconcile our theologies with the theologies of other traditions. On the other hand, we need real-life examples of how to live in the midst of pluralism. This chapter offers a call to the former and a depiction of the latter. The stories that follow are about three men who are deeply religious, who come from different faith traditions—one Muslim, one Jewish, and one Christian—and who demonstrate how rigorous academic scholarship contributes to the common good.[3] They provide a framework for thinking about pluralism that is rooted in religious conviction; in doing so, they

---

[2]Miroslav Volf, "A Common Word for a Common Future," in *A Common Word: Muslims and Christians on Loving God and Neighbor*, ed. Miroslav Volf, Ghazi bin Muhammad, and Melissa Yarrington (Grand Rapids: Eerdmans, 2010), 24.

[3]All of these individuals received the Templeton Prize, which is an award that Sir John Templeton established in 1972. Originally it was called the Templeton Prize for Progress in Religion, and initially Templeton thought that the prize should be given only to Christians. But he quickly concluded that he ought to honor great spiritual leaders of all faith traditions. Importantly, he did not want to honor and reward those who were known for their humanitarian efforts, their practical works, or their evangelism. Rather, he was interested in progress. Who had broken new ground in theology? What scholars and even practitioners had transformed the way we think about religious belief and practice? In Templeton's view, Alfred Nobel had missed an opportunity to recognize that progress in religion was possible and that many noteworthy individuals ought to be recognized for their significant contributions to human flourishing through the growth and expansion of religion, religious beliefs, and religious practice. Templeton created the Templeton Prize, and he set the amount higher than that of an individual Nobel Prize, to celebrate the "marvelous new things going on in religion." It is, in fact, an example of how philanthropy can draw attention to important topics and raise awareness of issues that deserve attention. See William Proctor, *The Templeton Touch* (New York: Doubleday, 1983).

demonstrate why pluralism, given the nature of human freedom and diversity, really is best for the common good.

King Abdullah II of the Hashemite Kingdom of Jordan

In 2018, King Abdullah II of the Hashemite Kingdom of Jordan received the forty-eighth Templeton Prize in a regal ceremony at the National Cathedral in Washington, DC. Abdullah was nominated for and was selected to receive the Templeton Prize because of his efforts to cultivate peace within the various factions in Islam and between Islam and Christianity. In 2004 he published *The Amman Message*, a response to the growing hostility toward Muslims as a result of the events that took place on September 11, 2001. Abdullah hoped to ease the tensions within Islam by articulating the common ground between the different legal schools within Islam, advocating for a broad definition of what it means to be Muslim, and arguing that declarations of apostasy should be abandoned.

In 2007, Abdullah extended his hand of reconciliation outside the Muslim tradition by supporting and funding the writing and the publication of "A Common Word Between Us and You." The document, which was cosigned by 138 Muslim scholars and opinion leaders, sought to ease the tensions that had emerged in response to Pope Benedict's speech in Regensburg, Germany, in 2006, in which he quoted a Byzantine emperor's comments about the "evil and inhuman" nature of Islam. With a call for peace between Muslims and Christians, "A Common Word" was written to counter the narrative of impending conflict between Muslim and Christian countries, a narrative that came to life in Samuel P. Huntington's *Clash of Civilizations and the Remaking of World Order*, Francis Fukuyama's *The End of History and the Last Man*, and Robert Kaplan's 1994 article

"The Coming Anarchy." According to Prince Ghazi bin Muhammad of Jordan, the goal of "A Common Word" was very clear.

> We wanted—and want—to avoid a greater worldwide conflict between Muslims and the West. We wanted to—and must—resolve all our current crises. To do both, we had—and have—to find a *modus vivendi* to live and let live, to "love thy neighbor"; this idea must be expressed from within our religious scriptures, and must then be applied everywhere.[4]

This modus vivendi emerged from two tenets that both Muslims and Christians (and in fact many faith traditions, including especially the Jewish faith tradition) share in common. The first is love of God. "A Common Word" opens with a ten-page explication of the Muslim teachings on love of God. Rooted in the Muslim emphasis on the preeminence of God, "there is no god but God," and in Muhammad's teaching that God's "is the sovereignty and His is the phrase and He hath power over all things," "A Common Word" explains the relationship between each phrase in Muhammad's teachings and the Muslim command to love God above all else. It is a careful treatment of the subject with detailed footnotes and references to the Qur'an. The next three pages of the text draw from the Bible, "You shall love the LORD your God with all your heart, with all your soul, and with all your strength" (Deuteronomy 6:4-5 NKJV). "A Common Word" cites Jesus and various texts from the Gospels and concludes that "the Prophet Muhammad was perhaps, through inspiration, restating and alluding to the Bible's First Commandment."[5]

---

[4]Ghazi bin Muhammad, "On 'A Common Word Between Us and You,'" in Volf, Bin Muhammad, and Yarrington, *Common Word*, 8. He also references the books cited in this paragraph (p. 4); these references are his and not my own.
[5]Bin Muhammad, "Common Word," 42.

That is really a remarkable claim. It draws a direct line between Judaism and Christianity, the two older monotheist faiths, and Islam. Prince Ghazi brings this to light a bit further in a book assessing the significance of "A Common Word." He tells the story of a young Muhammad, who attracts the attention of a Christian monk as the Prophet travels through the desert. Wherever the Prophet goes, whether walking or sitting, he is shielded from the sun by a cloud or a tree. Seeing this, and after conversing with the boy, the monk concludes that he has come into contact with a "Prophet among the Arabs, who were descended from Ishmael"; it's a reasonable conclusion according to Ghazi because both Genesis (Genesis 49:10) and Deuteronomy (Deuteronomy 18:15) intimate that a prophet who is not the Messiah and not from the tribe of Judah, but who is from the larger Jewish family, will emerge to lead the children of Ishmael.[6] The implication is this: although some might predict a coming conflagration between Muslims and Christians, there is a better way that is deeply rooted in a common spiritual heritage.

We find further commonality, according to the authors of "A Common Word," in the shared commitment to loving one's neighbor. "There are numerous injunctions in Islam about the necessity and paramount importance of love for—and mercy toward—the neighbor." Although this section is much shorter than the first, on love of God, the message is clear. Muhammad says, "None of you has faith until you love for your neighbor what you love for yourself," which mirrors Jesus's injunction to love your neighbor as you love yourself.[7]

"A Common Word" ends with a call to "come to a common word between us and you," and it compares teachings from the Qur'an

---

[6]Bin Muhammad, "Common Word," 15-16.
[7]Bin Muhammad, "Common Word," 43-44.

with words from the Bible to demonstrate what we have in common. "It is not simply," the authors of "A Common Word" say, "a matter for polite ecumenical dialogue."[8] The call to a common word is about the survival of humankind and the world in which we live.

In that regard, "A Common Word" is a conciliatory gesture to those outside the Muslim tradition. But King Abdullah took this message well beyond the printed word. In 2010, he proposed the creation of a World Interfaith Harmony Week, a proposal that was ultimately adopted as a resolution by the United Nations to be celebrated the first week of February. He opened Jordan to Syrian refugees. He worked with Mahmoud Abbas to reaffirm Abdullah's role as the custodian of Muslim and Christian holy sites, including the Church of the Holy Sepulchre. He secured the designation of the baptism site of Jesus Christ as a World Heritage Site and set aside land so that various Christian denominations could build churches on the site. He welcomed Pope Francis to Jordan, and at the Templeton Prize ceremony in 2018 he announced his intention to use the prize money for renovations at the Church of the Holy Sepulchre. These are remarkable acts for a Muslim head of state who must work very hard to balance the varied interests within his own country and faith tradition. Yet, as the protector of many Christian holy sites, Abdullah took the charge seriously.

He is motivated to do so because of his faith. "A Common Word" is an articulation of how the Muslim faith enjoins Muslims to love and serve their neighbor, even their non-Muslim neighbor, and that is why I believe Abdullah has served as benefactor for "A Common Word." At the same time, "A Common Word" is not a treatise on human rights rooted in an abstract notion of the common good.

---

[8]Bin Muhammad, "Common Word," 20, 25.

Rather, it draws from religious teachings; it finds the source of its moral imperative in religious belief and practice. This is in part a vision of the common good that becomes more relevant in an age where pluralism defines our life together.

Rabbi Lord Jonathan Sacks

But Abdullah represents just one example. In 2016, the Templeton Prize was awarded to Rabbi Lord Jonathan Sacks for his ability to build friendships with other faith leaders and to promote the "dignity of difference." As chief rabbi in the United Kingdom, he revitalized Jewish belief and practice through careful scholarship and a concerted effort to reflect publicly on contemporary issues. The most important theme throughout all of his writings deals with the challenges of living in a pluralistic age. *The Dignity of Difference*, published in 2002, captures the essence of Sacks's concern. The book, which was conceived of well before the events of September 11, 2001, but which went to print in a world transformed by religious violence, seeks a different way forward. However, it is more than a message of peace; it is a call, not unlike Abdullah's in "A Common Word," for the various faith traditions to reframe the way they understand and interpret their differences.

While Sacks finished *The Dignity of Difference*, he took an interest in the crisis facing the world's monotheistic faiths. Was it possible for Judaism, Islam, and Christianity to coexist and to become a source of peace and reconciliation instead of a justification for misguided politics and international brinksmanship? Seeking an answer to this question, Sacks started drafting a new book, which he did not publish until 2015. *Not in God's Name* extends Sacks's thesis in *The Dignity of Difference*. "We have little choice," Sacks writes in the introduction, "but to reexamine the theology that leads to violent conflict in the first place." In this book, Sacks offers a "Theology of the Other," a way of thinking about the continued existence of the Muslim, Jewish, and Christian faiths.[9]

The argument in *Not in God's Name* provides a framework for thinking about interfaith understanding. The writing and revision of the book exemplifies the best in interfaith relationships. Even though Sacks began to think about the book's content in the years that followed the events of September 11, 2001, he did not feel ready to publish it in the first decade of the twenty-first century, sensing his argument was not yet satisfactory.[10] He returned to the topic ten years later in response to the rise of the Islamic State. Then he sent the revised manuscript to Muslim, Jewish, and Christian colleagues, including N. T. Wright, the former bishop of Durham. The comments Sacks received from Wright led him to rewrite the section on Paul. He field-tested these ideas in lectures, even as he finished writing. In some of his talks, he told the story of Hagar and Ishmael. He offered a new way of interpreting a story from the Hebrew Bible that had shaped the kinship between Jews, Christians, and Muslims. The feedback he received suggested his perspective might make a valuable contribution to the conversation.

This is important because, in *Not in God's Name*, Sacks reinterprets the story of Hagar and Ishmael. Sacks offers a very different telling of Hagar's story, and it requires an open mind to consider the implications of his reinterpretation. As I attempt to summarize Sacks's exposition, I hope that you appreciate, as I did, the care with which he tested his argument with colleagues from the Christian tradition. Two important points are relevant to this discussion:

---

[9]Jonathan Sacks, *Not in God's Name: Confronting Religious Violence* (New York: Schocken, 2015), 25.

[10]Jonathan Sacks, email message to author, August 29, 2019.

(1) Sacks is a serious-minded scholar who believes that the answers to the difficult questions religion faces in the twenty-first century must be found in our religious texts, and (2) our religious traditions and the scholarship that emerges from religious belief and practice must be the foundation of every effort to define the common good.

With this in mind, Sacks returns to the texts that have troubled the relationship between Islam, Christianity, and Judaism. He reminds us that in many ways Genesis is a book about sibling rivalry—Cain and Abel, Isaac and Ishmael, and Jacob and Esau. In the latter two stories, God's promise is given to one and not the other brother, suggesting that the descendants of Ishmael and Esau have no place in God's plan. They are objects of the curse and not of blessing.

Sacks encourages us to study these stories in more detail. First, he notes that the Bible says Ishmael will be blessed four times—two promises given to Hagar, in Genesis 16:9-10; 21:17-20, and two promises to Abraham, in Genesis 17:20; 21:12-13. Ishmael may not be the father of the Jews, but he receives a promise nonetheless. God cares for Ishmael as he does for Isaac.[11]

Second, the story elicits empathy for Hagar and Ishmael. In many ways, Hagar is mistreated by Sarah, and we feel badly for her. "This is what gives the story its counter intuitive depth," Sacks writes. "At the first critical juncture for the covenantal family—the birth of its first children—we feel for Abraham and Sarah. . . . But we also feel for Hagar and Ishmael. We enter their world, see through their eyes, empathize with their emotions."[12] This twist of emotion leaves us to wonder, and in fact Sacks concludes with this point, whether it is possible for God to choose one without fully rejecting the other.

---

[11]Sacks, *Not in God's Name*, 110-11.
[12]Sacks, *Not in God's Name*, 118.

Finally, Sacks says the story of Isaac and Ishmael reaches an interesting conclusion in Genesis 25 (Genesis 25:8-9), when both Isaac and Ishmael attend Abraham's burial. Jewish tradition concludes that the two sons were brought together after Sarah's death because Abraham actually marries Hagar. If Genesis reports that Isaac and Ishmael attend their father's burial, we might infer that the two respected a common set of norms and that they may even have become reconciled to some degree.

A similar theme plays out in the story of Jacob and Esau, and of Joseph's enslavement in Egypt. In each case, a wrong is perpetrated by Jacob against Esau, and Joseph's brothers against Joseph; in both cases, there is grace and resolution. The wrongs are made right, the families reunite, and no one faces ultimate rejection. This is the key point. At the beginning of the book, Sacks notes that sibling rivalry characterizes the relationship between Jews, Christians, and Muslims. Who is the rightful heir? What religion has the truth? Who will find a place in God's kingdom? The purpose of *Not in God's Name* is to tell a different story. Instead of seeing Genesis as a tale of who wins, we should see the stories as a manifestation of God's love. Divine love is "governed by the principle of plenitude. . . . God does not prove his love for some by hating (and rejecting) others. Neither," says Sacks, "may we . . . if we follow him."[13]

In this way, Sacks articulates a vision of the common good, and not just for the individual communities but for the world, since the majority of its inhabitants belong to one of these three religious traditions. Importantly, it is a vision rooted in scholarly analysis, and Sacks has continued the argument in various contexts since publishing *Not in God's Name*. Religion is not going away. In fact, for a

---

[13]Sacks, *Not in God's Name*, 172-73.

variety of reasons Sacks argues that religion will become even more important in the twenty-first century.

In one way, according to Sacks, that possibility is positive in nature. Religion, after all, provides a sense of identity, purpose, and meaning. Religious communities form the basis for robust social networks, which can serve as a bulwark against loneliness, isolation, and individualism. And religious traditions are arguably one of the most global enterprises in the world today.[14]

But the growth of religious belief and practice also poses a risk. If religious people focus on the differences between their faith traditions, instead of what their traditions share in common, they will define themselves according to those distinctions. If religious adherents define their theology based on contemporary geopolitics, they might see a role for violence and extreme political positions as a way to protect and defend their faith. In these ways, religion could continue to foment division and violence.[15]

Sacks seeks another way. In a compelling speech at the American Academy of Religion in November 2016, Sacks challenged the scholars in attendance to use their craft for the good of the world. He told those gathered, "Never before has your work been more vital." Sacks said their task was to recover and to promote religious literacy, to teach the nuance found within all religious texts, and to understand the context in which the religious texts came to be. In teaching religious literacy, scholars must also help those who interpret to see the text as it might be read by others within their faith tradition as well as those outside their faith tradition. "Then comes the further task, maybe a theological one, of thinking through

---

[14]Jonathan Sacks, "Faith in the Future: The Promise and Perils of Religion in the 21st Century," The Office of Rabbi Sacks, November 30, 2016, http://rabbisacks.org/faith-future-promise -perils-religion.

[15]Sacks, "Faith in the Future."

what it means to live in the conscious presence of difference, of people whose narratives and texts are so different and yet [who] have to learn to co-exist. And then perhaps to recover a historical sense of how religion has acted in the past to resolve or mitigate conflict."[16]

Thus we see another articulation of the common good rooted in a religiously motivated vision of the world. Abdullah advocates a vision that recognizes what faith traditions hold in common—love of God and love of neighbor. Sacks takes this idea a bit further by calling for a faithful reinterpretation of those aspects of faith that divide us. Our religious ideals spring from our sacred texts, and where those texts suggest that conflict must characterize the relationship between faith traditions, Sacks asks whether we can, without violating their integrity, reread our scriptures in light of the "way the world is" in the twenty-first century.

These are perhaps hard words for the average evangelical Christian, because evangelicals cling to certain truths as a mark of being evangelical. But if the world becomes even more religious in the twenty-first century, it is also going to become more Muslim, more Jewish, and perhaps more broadly spiritual. How do evangelicals live in the midst of that? What are evangelical scholars called to do?

Professor Alvin Plantinga

The final vignette in this chapter is a story of the common good lived out in the life of one individual who pursued his work with conviction and grace. In 2017 the John Templeton Foundation honored Alvin Plantinga, the John A. O'Brien Professor of Philosophy Emeritus at the University of Notre Dame, with the Templeton Prize. For those of us who knew his work, we were thrilled. Plantinga has made an indelible mark on academic philosophy, and it was time

---

[16]Sacks, "Faith in the Future."

that a prize that focuses on celebrating the "spiritual dimension of human life" recognize a philosophical giant.

As many of you know, Plantinga does not directly engage, at least not in any public way, with the major geopolitical issues of our day. He is a Reformed Protestant who finds no reason to doubt God, even as he excels in his philosophical work. He argues that it is perfectly reasonable for a philosopher who believes in God to begin with that presupposition. If you take God's existence as a given, then you can think deeply about a wide range of philosophical issues, and, as Plantinga proved in his work, you can make good progress on some of the more complicated philosophical questions.

In this way, Plantinga exemplifies how a responsible defense of a particular position—in his case, of the rationality of the Christian faith—need not stand in opposition to the pursuit of the common good. If such defense is done with a humble commitment to reason and truth, as well as to respect and kindness toward others, advocacy for a particular position is compatible with, and is even indispensable to, the search for the common good.

But his scholarship is not the only reason I include Plantinga in my list of individuals who represent a certain vision of the common good. Plantinga has earned respect from fellow philosophers, including those who are religious and those who do not believe that religious belief is rational, because he makes very good philosophical arguments. As he says in the video that accompanies the announcement of the 2017 Templeton Prize, he has tried to be very thorough in his argumentation. And he is. But he is also very kind.

Dean Zimmerman, professor of philosophy at Rutgers University, writes this in his letter of recommendation on behalf of Plantinga's nomination:

What would be less evident to outsiders is the extent to which this renaissance was powered and shaped by Plantinga's personal gifts—his charm when engaging initially unsympathetic (or at least bewildered) peers, and his gentle, fatherly mentoring of generations of younger scholars. He has left his mark on hundreds of professors, who will always aspire to a small measure of the virtues he exemplifies. Chief among these virtues: confidence that God is a noble object of inquiry; . . . a deep humility toward the truth and toward the intellectual gifts of others, including one's staunchest critics; and a gentle manner with one's students, and even when dealing with belligerent opponents.[17]

Zimmerman's comments reflect something that became very clear to me as I learned more about Plantinga's work and contributions. To be sure, Plantinga has transformed the discipline of philosophy because he challenges the morass of logical positivism and the epistemological assumptions of his day. But he is also widely known as a fair and gracious interlocutor.

In a different reference letter written for Plantinga's nomination, Thomas Nagel, professor of philosophy and law emeritus at New York University, has this to offer:

He is consistently fair to opposing views and arguments, and he presents his own arguments with admirable clarity. . . . As someone without religious beliefs or even a religious background, I am extremely grateful to him for treating this subject with a clarity and cogency that makes it accessible to anyone prepared to approach it with an open mind and the universal resources of reason.[18]

---

[17]Dean Zimmerman to the John Templeton Foundation, September 18, 2012.
[18]Thomas Nagel to the John Templeton Foundation, November 1, 2012.

It is this spirit of grace that characterizes all three of the men discussed in this chapter. Abdullah is the consummate statesman who opens the borders of his country to the outcast and downtrodden, and protects the life of faith for all religious believers in Jordan. Sacks is a religious leader who befriended Christian leaders when he served as chief rabbi and seeks to build bridges with other faith leaders whenever possible. Plantinga is a scholar who knows that the effectiveness of an argument also lays in the way it is delivered and how refutations are handled. Each has found friendship within and well beyond their particular faith traditions. None of these individuals has forsaken his tradition in doing so. In that regard, Abdullah, Sacks, and Plantinga model a vision of the common good for our time.

This last point is particularly important. We live in a global community where the world's religions come into contact on a regular basis; the landscape of religious belief and practice is changing dramatically, and all of us will find ourselves living next to or working with many deeply religious people who share a commitment to faith but who may follow a different religious tradition.

The Humble Approach

Abdullah, Sacks, and Plantinga demonstrate that we do not have to give up our beliefs to live in harmony with our non-Christian neighbors. John Inazu, the Sally D. Danforth Distinguished Professor of Law and Religion and professor of political science at Washington University in St. Louis, calls this confident pluralism. In his book bearing the same title, Inazu writes, "Our shared existence is not only possible but also necessary." We live in a pluralistic age, and

> confident pluralism takes both confidence (in our religious
> beliefs) and pluralism ("the recognition that we live in a society
> of a plurality of conflicting and incommensurable" religious

and non-religious views) seriously. . . . Confident pluralism allows genuine difference to coexist without suppressing or minimizing our firmly held convictions.[19]

But, you may ask, is that even possible? Can we really extend the hand of friendship through mutual understanding to those outside our faith tradition and still believe in the tenets of our own tradition? Jews do not believe that Jesus is the Messiah. Muslims will not ever accept that Jesus was divine in any way. Christians will always maintain that salvation is found in Christ alone. The differences are seemingly intractable unless we take a different approach. Let us call it the humble approach.

The Humble Approach is the name of a book written by Sir John Templeton, the benefactor of the Templeton philanthropies, to explain his philanthropic vision.[20] In the opening pages, Templeton "reminds us that each person's concept of God, the universe, even his or her own self is too limited." His chief concern is this: religious people rarely admit that they might be wrong; those with strong religious convictions build theologies that demand certainty when so much of religious belief depends on faith.

Inazu makes this same point in his book. While noting that religious people should retain their core convictions, Inazu writes about epistemic humility. "Humility is a reminder of the limits of translation, and the difficulty of proving our deeply held values to one another." Citing British theologian and missionary Lesslie Newbigin, who wrote, "We are continually required to act on beliefs that are not

---

[19]John Inazu, *Confident Pluralism: Surviving and Thriving Through Deep Difference* (Chicago: University of Chicago Press, 2016), 4, 6-7.

[20]John Templeton created three grant-making entities to carry out his philanthropic vision: the John Templeton Foundation (www.templeton.org), the Templeton World Charity Foundation (www.templetonworldcharity.org), and the Templeton Religion Trust (www.templetonreligiontrust.org).

demonstrably certain and to commit our lives to propositions that can be doubted," Inazu contends that our inability to irrefutably demonstrate the key aspects of our religious beliefs "should lead us to a more humble posture in our engagement with others."[21]

Miroslav Volf concurs. "God, who dwells in inapproachable light," Volf writes, "is never fully present in the consciousness and practice of the faithful, even the most enlightened ones."[22] Therefore, humility includes recognizing one's limitations and accepting that people of other faiths and even those without faith can enlighten and inform one's personal convictions.

This is, in one sense, what it means to live comfortably within a pluralist reality. Religion is not dead. "Secularization theory," according to Peter Berger, the great sociologist of religion and a former proponent of that theory, "can no longer be maintained in the face of empirical evidence"; as a result, scholars must rethink the place of religion in the twenty-first century. "We need a theory of pluralism," writes Berger in his 2014 book *The Many Altars of Modernity*, and it is not "an obscure, impractical exercise."[23] The challenges that Sacks addresses in his work and that Abdullah manages through political leadership are not academic concerns. But both men, and many other leaders like them, need scholarship to inform policies, programs, and decisions. Christians are asking, "What should be the main concern of Christ's followers when it comes to living well in the world today?"[24] Muslims are wondering, "What could and

---

[21]Inazu, *Confident Pluralism*, 89-90. Inazu draws this conclusion in a section where he defines the concept of humility. See Lesslie Newbigin, *Proper Confidence: Faith, Doubt, and Certainty in Christian Discipleship* (Grand Rapids: Eerdmans, 1995).

[22]Miroslav Volf, *A Public Faith: How Followers of Christ Should Serve the Common Good* (Grand Rapids: Brazos, 2011), 112-13.

[23]Peter Berger, *The Many Altars of Modernity: Toward a Paradigm for Religion in a Pluralist Age* (Boston: Walter de Gruyter, 2014), ix.

[24]Volf, *Public Faith*, xvii.

should an Islamic modernity look like?"[25] Similarly, evangelical scholars have both the opportunity and responsibility to think critically about the place of religious practice and belief in a world where good people of many different faith traditions share the same zip code, attend the same schools, and worship within blocks of one another. How then should we live?

The first response to that question for evangelical scholars requires a deeper appreciation for pluralism. In *The Many Altars of Modernity*, Berger attempts to formulate a "new paradigm." But, as Berger notes, "much more work will be needed to flesh it out. . . . It will require efforts over some years by colleagues from different disciplines and with different competencies."[26] *Faith in a Pluralist Age* answers Berger's call by bringing together a collection of responses from evangelical scholars to Berger's claim that pluralism is not only a mark of modernity; pluralism is also good for all religions and specifically for the Christian tradition. This is a challenging claim. Does a positive perspective of pluralism negate the need for evangelism? Does pluralism require that evangelicals give up their beliefs or dilute their convictions so that their faith becomes bland? Does not pluralism weaken rather than strengthen religious commitments? Berger's analysis offers some answers.

He makes three points ("three theological benefits"), which are summarized in his contribution to *Faith in a Pluralist Age*, having been previously developed in *The Many Altars of Modernity*. First, the pluralist context that characterizes religion in the twenty-first century elevates the role of faith in religious commitment and belief. This point reflects some of what Inazu and Volf have argued. "Sola fide . . . the battle cry of the Protestant Reformation . . . denotes

---

[25]Berger, *Many Altars*, xi.
[26]Berger, *Many Altars*, xi.

acceptance of the penumbra of doubt that goes with faith that no longer is taken for granted."[27] To say that true belief must eradicate all doubt is to ignore a core component of the human experience.

Similarly, pluralism makes the church a "voluntary association." There is simply more choice, and while many would struggle with the view that communities of faith are just one option in the market-place of ideas, pluralism requires that we accept a new role for the church or one's particular denomination. The end result of this new reality may make one's faith commitment stronger and, in that re-spect, more real.

Finally, pluralism encourages people of faith to distinguish "the non-negotiable core of faith from more peripheral features."[28] Here too, while the implications of this conclusion might be unsettling, Berger encourages us to see the benefits. When we live in a world where different faith traditions interact on a regular basis and where the congregants in all of these groups are good people who seek the common good for their community, nation, and the world, we have to find a way to make sense of our differences. Berger provides a way to think about the reality of pluralism, and in doing so he shows how pluralism can strengthen and deepen religious faith.[29] How then shall we live?

---

[27]Peter Berger, "Faith in a Pluralist Age," in *Faith in a Pluralist Age*, ed. Kaye V. Cook (Eugene, OR: Cascade Books, 2018), 9.

[28]Berger, *Faith in a Pluralist Age*, 13.

[29]See Berger, "Faith in a Pluralist Age," 9-16, for a full articulation of Berger's analysis. He ends his chapter with the following: "Pluralism has benefits for faith. The reflection toward which it pushes believers is also beneficial, on every level of sophistication, because it deepens the question of what I myself—and not just some abstract community to which I am supposed to belong—really believes" (16). On the other hand, it is worth noting that pluralism may actually weaken faith. Berger also recognizes this: "Religious conservatives argue that plural-ism relativizes the affirmations of faith. There is no denying that they have a point." More-over, "The Apostle Paul was right on this: Sustained conversations with unbelievers threatens alleged religious certainties. Fundamentalism is the project to prevent such conversation" (3, 8). These points further demonstrate what scholars and practitioners might contribute to a new paradigm. Does pluralism weaken or strengthen faith? Would a deeper appreciation

Another response to this question goes far beyond the academy and into the hearts and minds of men and women. In fact, Berger recognizes that the scholarly enterprise can go only so far. "A general insight of sociology," he writes, "is that every institution, if it is to function in society, must be internalized in the minds of individuals."[30] It is not enough to theorize about pluralism; pluralism must be lived out in how we interact with others. Pluralism, after all, is the reality of the modern era, and in that regard it is also the vision of the common good for the twenty-first century. Pluralism allows religious belief to flourish; pluralism allows religious traditions of all kinds to flourish, and pluralism will lead to new insights, new efforts, and new practices that unite people from many different backgrounds in service to the common good.

The opportunity for evangelical scholars rests in articulating that vision for the evangelical community; the opportunity for public intellectuals rests in communicating the ways in which pluralism is not only good for religion but also good for evangelicalism. The opportunity for evangelicals is to put the work of the scholars and the words of the intellectuals into action. This is where the examples of Rabbi Sacks, King Abdullah, and Professor Alvin Plantinga speak to the age in which we live. In each case, they have built friendships with those who do not see the world or practice faith as these men do. But their personal friendships and their acts of generosity have taken theory beyond the written word and helped to internalize it in hearts and minds. We should go and do likewise.

---

for pluralism mitigate the worst effects of fundamentalism? How does one retain core convictions and respect the faith of others?

[30]Berger, *Many Altars*, 60.

5

The Common Grace of
Journalism in a Post-Truth Era

Katelyn Beaty

"I can tell you this. We are putting out a damn paper tomorrow."[1] So declared reporter Chase Cook the day that a man armed with a pump-action shotgun stormed into the offices of the *Capital Gazette* with the intent to kill as many people as possible. There were eleven people in the Annapolis, Maryland, newsroom that day. Five of them were killed in the attack. The shooter, later charged with first-degree murder, had long harangued the newspaper staff after it had reported on harassment charges made against him. And yet the next morning, the paper went out as Cook had said it would: The front-page story reported on the shooting. The opinion page was left blank except for the names of the five who were slain. To put the paper out, staff members camped out with their laptops in a parking garage across the street from the offices. *Capital Gazette* editor Jimmy DeButts wrote that he was "devastated and heartbroken" over the event, but said this regarding his work:

---

[1]Chase Cook (@chaseacook), "I can tell you this: We are putting out a damn paper tomorrow," Twitter, June 28, 2018, 6:38 p.m., https://twitter.com/chaseacook/status/1012465236195061766.

There are no 40 hour weeks, no big paydays—just a passion for telling stories from our community. . . .

We try to expose corruption. We fight to get access to public records & bring to light the inner workings of government despite major hurdles put in our way. The reporters & editors put their all into finding the truth.[2]

They put their all into "finding the truth." If you are a cynical reader of the news, fed on a steady diet of spin and sensationalism, you might respond as Pontius Pilate did in his discourse with Jesus: "What is truth?" (John 18:38 NIV). Pilate despaired of the truth, and so do we. Can any of us really claim to know and convey the full truth? Doesn't the truth look different depending on whom you ask? When the who, what, where, when, and why of a story differ wildly from one storyteller to another, whom do we trust to tell us the truth?

These are all timely questions in our post-truth era. The 2016 Word of the Year for Oxford Dictionaries was *post-truth*. It is a time when "objective facts are less influential in shaping public opinion than appeals to emotion and personal belief."[3] In a post-truth era, it seems audacious if not foolish for the *Capital Gazette* and hundreds of newspapers like it across the country to keep on putting their all into finding the truth when many of their readers are not sure it exists. Yet for Christian leaders and scholars working in a post-truth era, journalism provides a model of serving the common good, however beleaguered and shaky the enterprise seems to be in this cultural and political moment.

---

[2]Kristen Hare, "Capital Gazette Journalist on Twitter: 'Please Understand, We Do All This to Serve Our Community,'" Poynter, June 28, 2018, www.poynter.org/newsletters/2018/capital-gazette-journalist-on-twitter-please-understand-we-do-all-this-to-serve-our-community.
[3]"Word of the Year 2016," Oxford Dictionaries, accessed October 31, 2019, https://languages.oup.com/word-of-the-year/word-of-the-year-2016.

Despite individual journalists who sometimes get it wrong, journalism as an institution is critical to American common life. From this country's founding and secured in our constitutional law, a free press has helped citizens to access a free flow of information and ideas. It is one institution that holds other institutions, especially governmental bodies, accountable against corruption and tyranny. As a result, a free press is the envy of people living under repressive regimes worldwide. Journalists risk and sometimes sacrifice their lives to pursue truth over against the demagoguery of dictators and despots.

Among the recent martyrs of journalism is Jamal Khashoggi, named *Time* magazine's Person of the Year in 2018 alongside the *Capital Gazette* reporters.[4] Khashoggi was a Saudi Arabian journalist and *Washington Post* columnist who criticized the Saudi crown prince for, among other things, Saudi Arabia's involvement in the war in Yemen, a war that has claimed upwards of fifty thousand lives due to violence and famine. In October 2018, Khashoggi was reported to have been missing for a month after having arrived at a Saudi consulate in Istanbul. Then, in November, a Saudi public prosecutor announced that Khashoggi had been given a lethal injection inside the consulate and that his body had been dismembered. Such can be the cost of telling the truth when others do not want you to speak it.

The late Senator John McCain knew that when journalists are prevented from doing their job of pursuing the truth, all of us suffer. In 2017 he told CNN, "If you want to preserve democracy as we know it, you have to have a free and many times adversarial press." He continued, "And without it, I am afraid that we would lose so

---

[4]Karl Vick, "Time Person of the Year: The Guardians and the War on Truth," *Time*, December 11, 2018, https://time.com/person-of-the-year-2018-the-guardians.

much of our individual liberties over time. That's how dictators get started."[5] But journalism is about more than preventing dictators from cropping up, as important as that task is. When journalists attempt, however imperfectly, to report the truth about our cities, our nation, and our world, they lay the groundwork for understanding God's redemptive activity in it.

From a spiritual perspective, good journalists bear witness to the way that sin and evil have marred God's world and God's image bearers. But they also often witness to the ways that seeds of redemption are being sown in the unlikeliest of places, industries, and communities. Journalists remind us that *this* world is the arena of God's redemptive activity, and that the Father in his graciousness has poured out common grace on unlikely servants to restrain the full effects of sin and corruption. When I open up the Sunday *New York Times* or get a news alert from the Associated Press, I am confident that what I read will bear witness to how broken we are, how badly the whole human enterprise needs redemption. Yet I also hope and anticipate that I will see evidence of how God in Christ is working through individuals and institutions to bring healing to the nations. Christians should read the headlines anticipating that the God of the universe will show up in them, for even the headlines belong to him.

As a journalist, editor, and Christ-follower, I want to give voice to the importance of journalism in a post-truth era, as well as name a few virtues that Christian scholars can learn from good journalists. It may strike you as an inauspicious time to do so. Trust in the media—trust that journalists are providing a fair, balanced, and corroborated account of reality—has perhaps never been

---

[5]Eugene Scott, "McCain: Dictators 'Get Started by Suppressing Free Press,'" CNN, February 20, 2017, www.cnn.com/2017/02/18/politics/john-mccain-donald-trump-dictators/index.html.

lower. Gallup found that from 2003 to 2016, the percentage of Americans who said they have a great or fair amount of trust in the media fell from 54 to 32 percent. Of those who said they had lost trust in that time, a full 30 percent said their trust in the media could not be restored.[6] Both conservatives and liberals say they have lost trust, although the mistrust runs deeper among Americans who identify as conservative and who see a liberal bias among major news outlets.

That mistrust has spurred a proliferation of news outlets that counter other outlets' blind spots and spin. That any of us can choose news sources that confirm our ideological biases—and we all have them—both reflects and perpetuates the deep polarization of our time. It was once the case that Americans read or watched the same three or four major news outlets. In the UK, the BBC had an even more limited offering. Together, these outlets provided a common national narrative and, by extension, a shared national identity. Today, all of us can choose to get only the news that confirms our biases and keeps us in ideological silos.

Distrust of news media is strong among American evangelicals, who rightly perceive that their beliefs, practices, and daily life are often misunderstood and misrepresented. Even publications such as the *New York Times* and the *New Yorker* have proven track records of frequently getting evangelicals wrong, referring to them as "evangelists" or "the evangelicals," which is to miss the movement's decentralized nature and on-the-ground diversity. Religion remains a blind spot for many journalists, who seem to fill in the facts with stereotypes and hastily scanned Wikipedia pages. This leads to some errors that are by turns hilarious and grating.

---

[6]"Indicators of News Media Trust," Knight Foundation, September 11, 2018, https://knightfoundation.org/reports/indicators-of-news-media-trust.

One 2014 *New York Times* report on tourism to Israel noted that the Church of the Holy Sepulchre marks the site where "many Christians believe that Jesus is buried."[7] If many Christians really believe that Jesus' body is buried in the ground, the story should have been on the front page, since Christians have historically believed that Jesus was physically resurrected from the dead. (After reader scrutiny, the *Times* updated the story to read, "where many Christians believe that Jesus *was* buried" [emphasis mine].)

Journalists might have a particularly hard time getting evangelicals right, because evangelicalism is a diverse and global movement, drawing from hundreds of denominations, each with distinct emphases, traditions, and figureheads. It includes believers as diverse as Chinese house churches that meet in secret due to government restriction and Nigerian megachurches that draw two hundred thousand worshipers each week and blend faith with promises of financial success. When a reporter wants to know what Catholics think of a particular bill in the Senate, for example, she knows what search terms to Google and whom to call: a local archbishop, say, or a statement from the US Conference of Catholic Bishops. By contrast, evangelicals do not have a pope. In the vacuum of centralized leadership, often the loudest voices espousing the most extreme views end up speaking for the whole family to media outlets.

President Donald Trump has exploited Americans' mistrust of media, decrying reporting that casts him and his political allies in a negative light as "fake news." Indeed, he has gone so far as to call the press "the enemy of the people." That phrase is alarming not least because it is the language used by totalitarian leaders to describe anyone

---

[7]Matthew Kalman, "Hoping War-Weary Tourists Will Return to Israel," *New York Times*, September 16, 2014, www.nytimes.com/2014/09/21/travel/hoping-war-weary-tourists-will-return-to-israel.html/.

who challenges their regimes. Even conservative media have sounded the alarm about Trump's repeated attacks on the media. Still, there is a reason his language resonates with a segment of Americans.

I was traveling overseas in January 2019 when a video taken outside the Lincoln Memorial in Washington, DC, began appearing in my news feed. That video captured an encounter between a group of teenagers and a Native American activist. The activist, Nathan Phillips, was participating in an indigenous peoples' march the same weekend as the annual March for Life. The video shows Phillips playing a tribal drum while facing a teenager. The teen, Nick Sandmann, is smiling in a way that's hard to discern, but many who watched the video interpreted the smile as mocking. Phillips told reporters that boys in the group—from a Catholic high school in Covington, Kentucky—were chanting "build that wall" and doing tomahawk chops with their hands. Based on the initial video footage and Phillips's account, several media went forward with a story condemning the Covington Catholic students, and the public outcry was swift and fierce.

But then more footage emerged that complicated the story. A much longer video shows members of the Hebrew Israelites group hurling insults at the teenagers as well as the Native American activists. At one point in the video, Phillips moves into the crowd of boys, and Sandmann, the one whose smile had initially enraged so many, was now seen by many to be engaging Phillips with an attempt at peace. Then more reports: Phillips apparently had never been deployed to Vietnam, as many outlets had reported; this could have been confirmed by a call to the Pentagon. No footage of the boys saying "build that wall" was ever found. The apologies initially issued by Covington Catholic High School for the teens' behavior were replaced by apologies *to the teens*. And many commentators who had condemned the boys for their behavior backed off. To be sure, it's possible that the teens had been harassed by the Hebrew Israelites *and* had been mocking Phillips—both of these things can be true. But the media coverage of the encounter gave many of us ideological whiplash. It also continued to erode public trust that reporters at top institutions are doing due diligence.

If the Lincoln Memorial media blunder teaches us anything, it is that the truth cannot so easily be slotted into binary and strident ideological categories. Nor can the truth be rushed. Good journalism takes time. It requires getting on the phone with multiple sources, digging into public records, and backing up every claim with sourcing and fact checking. It means that if you cannot get sources on the phone or cannot confirm key elements of a story, you hold off on publishing a story—especially a story involving private citizens and minors, no less. The insider talk for this is, "The story's not there." And if the story's not there, you do not publish it.

Speed kills good journalism. And in a moment when both sides of the polarized public square rush to condemn the other side, the rules of journalism require you to refuse to play into ideological narratives when the on-the-ground truth is more complex. But when investigative journalists put in the long, hard work of digging into a complex story—and many of them do, every day—their work can be no less than a revelation and a balm.

In 2002, investigative reporters at the *Boston Globe* unveiled decades of sexual abuse by priests in the Catholic Archdiocese of Boston and the ways those priests had been protected by the church's highest leaders. Powerfully depicted in the Oscar Award–winning film *Spotlight*, the reporters spent months rifling through church directories, interviewing victims, petitioning courts to release sealed documents, even interviewing some of the priests accused of abuse. *Spotlight* makes clear that these journalists are imperfect vessels, and their work is tedious and unglamorous.

It is also worth remembering that murmurings about the larger sex-abuse scandal first broke in the *National Catholic Reporter* back in 1985, when other Catholic publications would not touch the story. Those early reports paved the way for the *Boston Globe* team, and the results of their reporting could not have been more earth shattering—the eventual unveiling of decades of coverup that many believe goes all the way to the Vatican. As an immediate result of the team's reporting, five priests were criminally prosecuted, and 552 victims and parents who had filed civil lawsuits were awarded $95 million in settlements—an imperfect justice, but justice nonetheless.[8]

Marty Baron, currently executive editor of the *Washington Post*, oversaw the Boston team when they broke the sex-abuse scandal. He had this to say upon receiving the Hitchens Award in 2016 for excellence in journalism:

> I was often asked how we at *The Boston Globe* were willing to take on the most powerful institution in New England and among the most powerful in the world, the Catholic Church.
>
> The question really mystifies me—especially when it comes from journalists or those who hope to enter the profession. Because holding the most powerful to account is what we are *supposed* to do. If we do not do that, then what exactly *is* the purpose of journalism? . . . The truth is not meant to be hidden. It is not meant to be suppressed. It is not meant to be ignored. It is not meant to be disguised. It is not meant to

---

[8]"Spotlight Investigation: Abuse in the Catholic Church," *Boston Globe*, 2002–2004, http://archive.boston.com/globe/spotlight/abuse/index.shtml.

be manipulated. It is not meant to be falsified. Otherwise, wrongdoing will persist.[9]

"The truth is not meant to be hidden." Baron's words call to mind Jesus' teaching in the Gospels. The Four Gospels arrive to us as eyewitness news of sorts, as collections of various accounts of firsthand experiences with an itinerant Galilean preacher who shared the good news during his public ministry in first-century Palestine. To be sure, many of the New Testament accounts of Jesus would not pass the veracity test of many modern newsrooms. Luke never corroborated the story of Zacchaeus, and, besides, he should have been specific about just how short Zacchaeus was. Further, if John is going to tell us only that "a great crowd of people" (John 6:2 NIV) was swarming Jesus, he can hardly print that there were in fact five thousand. Nonetheless, the Christian faith is unique among world religions in asking us to trust the accounts of people who encountered another person with a who, what, where, when, and why to his life, who also claimed to be the second person of the eternal triune God—in history and beyond it all at once.

According to the testimony of Luke (and of Matthew and Mark in slightly different iterations), Jesus says, "No one lights a lamp and hides it in a clay jar or puts it under a bed. Instead, they put it on a stand, so that those who come in can see the light. For there is nothing hidden that will not be disclosed, and nothing concealed that will not be known or brought out into the open" (Luke 8:16-17 NIV). Jesus is talking about the light of the good news, the news that Christ came into the world to save sinners, and that forgiveness and renewal of life are available to all who

---

[9]Martin Baron, "*Washington Post* Editor Marty Baron Has a Message to Journalists in the Trump Era," *Vanity Fair*, November 30, 2016, www.vanityfair.com/news/2016/11/washington-post-editor-marty-baron-message-to-journalists.

put their trust in him. But Jesus is also telling his followers not to resist the light of truth, because all people will stand in it one day, when all hearts will be fully known, open, and revealed for their true contents.

Thus, Jesus' words could be a life verse for journalists. At the least, good journalism can expose suffering, injustice, and exploitation of the vulnerable. It can bring dark things into the light and can spur institutions to do the same. If my Reformed education at Calvin College taught me anything, it is that God leaves traces of grace throughout the world, even among people who do not believe in God and would scoff at the notion that they are doing the Lord's work. As theologian Cornelius Plantinga Jr. writes, "God's Spirit works everywhere in the world to pour out good gifts on the merciful and unmerciful, on the grateful and ungrateful, on believers and unbelievers alike. God checks the spread of corruption by preserving in humanity a sense of divinity and the voice of conscience."[10] Good journalism is a measure of common grace insofar as it checks the spread of individual and institutional sin from having its full effects in the world. It is thus a gift.

It can be hard for us to receive this gift when the sin being reported is our own. I started my career at *Christianity Today* magazine, the flagship publication of evangelicalism, founded by Billy Graham in 1956. Over the nine-plus years that I worked there, we were sometimes required to report bad news about Christian leaders and organizations. We understood this to be an extension of the classic metaphor of journalism as holding up a mirror to a community. The purpose of the mirror is not to shame but to correct. Yet, as you might imagine, some of our readers did not want to look in

---

[10]Cornelius Plantinga Jr., *Engaging God's World: A Christian Vision of Faith, Learning, and Living* (Grand Rapids: Eerdmans, 2002), 59.

the mirror. (I would know because I had the glamorous role of reading the letters to the editor.)

In spring 2018, the *Chicago Tribune* broke a story about Willow Creek Community Church and allegations of sexual misconduct against its founding pastor. The *Tribune* went forward with the story after months of investigation and a sit-down interview with Bill Hybels.[11] The report resulted in Hybels's early retirement, and his two pastoral successors stepped down amid the fallout. Both *Christianity Today* and the *New York Times* published their own in-depth reports. In fact, leaders at the church had learned of the allegations before the *Tribune* broke the story, but the Willow Creek Association board had voted not to investigate the allegations when they came to light. This led several high-profile board members to resign. After the *Tribune* and *Christianity Today* went forward with detailed and balanced reports, Willow Creek leaders defended Hybels, then later apologized to the women who had come forward with allegations.

The truth is that *Christianity Today* had learned about the Willow Creek Association board resignations at least two years before the story broke and assigned a reporter to follow it closely. The editors put a lot of time and energy into getting the story right, because they knew the fallout, should the allegations prove to be credible, would be enormous among *Christianity Today* readers. Would not the millions of people who had heard Hybels's preaching, read his books, or otherwise trusted him to lead with integrity want to know if there was sinful or illegal behavior going on behind closed doors? Are not we called to hold spiritual leaders to a higher bar than we do other leaders?

---

[11]Manya Brachear Pashman and Jeff Coen, "After Years of Inquiries, Willow Creek Pastor Denies Misconduct Allegations," *Chicago Tribune*, March 23, 2018, www.chicagotribune.com /news/breaking/ct-met-willow-creek-pastor-20171220-story.html.

Unfortunately, not all Christians took the reporting in the manner in which it was intended. Many *Christianity Today* readers believed Hybels to be the victim of a "media takedown" in the #MeToo era and saw the reporting as secular journalists ravaging a godly man's character. Others simply did not believe the allegations or, if they did, just didn't think they were serious enough to warrant the headlines or recourse. And, naturally, anyone who was brought to Christ through Hybels's preaching or the ministry of Willow Creek found it difficult to square this positive, life-transforming experience with the image of a man using his power to abuse women in his midst.

But, if anything, the Willow Creek story suggests that Christian institutions are not immune from the corruption and abuse found in secular institutions. This truth should be easy for Christians of all people to acknowledge. The whole of Scripture and the story of God's people show that the human heart is a muddled thing, that all of us are *simil iustus et peccator*—saints and sinners alike. As the apostle Paul says, "For I have the desire to do what is good, but I cannot carry it out. For I do not do the good I want to do, but the evil I do not want to do—this I keep on doing" (Romans 7:18-19 NIV). Or, as Russian novelist Alekandr Solzenhitsyn writes, "The line separating good and evil passes not through states, nor between classes, nor between political parties either—but right through every human heart—and through all human hearts."[12]

Good journalism shows us the evil that can lurk even in holy institutions, in ways that we cannot always see when we are invested in them. Part of the reason we cannot always see problems in our midst is that we often benefit from it going unchecked. Journalism

---

[12]Aleksandr Solzhenitsyn, *The Gulag Archipelago 1918–1956: An Experiment in Literary Investigation*, vol. 1 (New York: Basic Books, 1997).

can stop us from putting Christian leaders on pedestals. It can help us see the truth when we do not want to.

When we read critical news about Christian leaders and institutions, many of us naturally assume a posture of defense or disbelief. Indeed, when *Christianity Today* reported on Willow Creek, several members of the church found the report hard to believe—not because it was inaccurate but because it did not accord with their positive experience in the church. But we might more readily receive such news as a strange grace, as an opportunity to reflect, repent, and reform. The church, after all, claims to be the clearest representative on earth of the God of the universe. God sets the bar exceedingly high for God's people, and so should we. The church is not supposed to be just like any other human institution. As media have continued to cover the Catholic Church amid news of ongoing abuse coverup, *New York Times* commentator Ross Douthat wrote, "The church is a target because it asks to be a target—because it aspires to set a higher standard, and answer to a higher master, than princes, governments and civic institutions." Douthat encourages fellow Catholics to receive the media scrutiny "as a spur to virtue and as a sign that their faith still matters, that their church still looms large over the affairs of men, and that the world still cares enough about Christianity to demand that Catholics live up to their own exacting standards."[13]

As God's people, we want to leave the aroma of Christ wherever we go. But sometimes outsiders sniff out a stench among us. Personally, if I smell bad and someone gently but clearly tells me that I am stinking up the place, I appreciate the feedback. Knowing that I smell helps to prevent future embarrassment and offending the

---

[13]Ross Douthat, "The Position of the Church," *New York Times*, March 29, 2010, https://douthat.blogs.nytimes.com/2010/03/29/the-position-of-the-church.

people sitting next to me. To use a more serious metaphor, if a medical scan reveals that I have a tumor that will become deadly if it is not immediately removed, my response is not to scoff at the technician or point out all the other body parts that are working just fine. The hard work remains of removing the tumor and recovering full health, but without that scan, I might not live much longer. I am grateful for the bad news, because it means I do not have to face worse news later.

Today we think of journalism as a secular enterprise, protected by key tenets of the Constitution. But it is worth noting that key journalistic principles, such as free speech, freedom of conscience, and political reform, arguably arose from Christian beliefs, those of Protestant voices in seventeenth-century England. In a fascinating book, *From Yahweh to Yahoo! The Religious Roots of the Secular Press*, journalism scholar Doug Underwood recounts how Puritan poet-scholar John Milton and George Fox, the founder of the Quaker movement, used pamphlets to express religious and political dissent in the public square. Newsbooks, as they were called, circulated among booksellers and included stories of political intrigue as well as theological salvos. Fox, in particular, used the printing press to issue pamphlets to challenge the state church and plead the cause of people trampled by injustice.[14] Fox understood himself to be working within the prophetic tradition, wherein prophets warn the Israelites about the consequences of neglecting God's calls to care for the poor and oppressed. We see a secularized version of this prophetic tradition when journalists hold the powerful to account and draw attention to injustice faced by fellow citizens who cannot speak for themselves.

---

[14]Doug Underwood, *From Yahweh to Yahoo!: The Religious Roots of the Secular Press*, The History of Communication (Champaign: University of Illinois Press, 2002).

Over and against the stereotypes of a godless media machine, it is worth noting that Christians are found in every major news organization in the country. Many Christians in the media, such as investigative reporter Marshall Allen, bring a sense of vocational calling to their daily work. Allen began his career on the health care beat at the *Las Vegas Sun*. He compiled data that showed that Nevada hospitals had the worst national rate of readmissions, meaning that many patients had to return to the hospital within thirty days of being discharged. The state had been gathering inpatient data for decades, but that data was well controlled by the hospitals and inaccessible to the public. Allen and his colleagues spent two years digging into the data, with the goal of helping citizens make informed decisions about medical treatment. Their research revealed inadequate staffing, flawed oversight, and patient abuse that in a few cases led to death. Reflecting on the investigation, Allen wrote,

> Some people might think that Christians are supposed to be soft and acquiescent rather than muckrakers who hold the powerful to account. But what I do as an investigative reporter is consistent with what the Bible teaches. The Bible teaches that people are made in the image of God and that each human life holds incredible value. So when I learned that medical mistakes are one of the leading causes of death in America, I called attention to the problem.[15]

When Allen started his career in Christian media, he wrote, he found resistance among editors to report bad news if the reporting cast Christian leaders in a negative light. But Allen reminds us that

---

[15]Marshall Allen, "The Biblical Guide to Reporting," *New York Times*, September 1, 2018, www.nytimes.com/2018/09/01/opinion/christianity-bible-journalism.html.

sometimes godly obedience looks like upsetting the powers that be, especially when human dignity is at stake.

Today, the administrations of some Christian colleges, notably Liberty University in Lynchburg, Virginia, insist on reviewing their student newspapers and occasionally pull stories that challenge the administration. Liberty's former president Jerry Falwell Jr. was known to review and sign off on every story in the *Liberty Champion*. Since 2016, he pulled articles that were critical of President Trump or that highlighted anti-Trump Christian leaders. In 2018, when students asked whether the review policy violated the basic principles of journalism, two editors were fired and several more resigned in protest. *Liberty Champion* staff today sign a nondisclosure agreement that prevents them from speaking on record when outside journalists want to report on Liberty. The students are also barred from using social media to share news from their school.[16] When Liberty and other Christian colleges create such strict review of student newspapers, they are training students to work at public-relations firms, not newsrooms. Public relations has its place, but once you treat a student newspaper like a marketing department, you have traded truth for propaganda.

Despite this discouraging example from Liberty, I believe Christian leaders and scholars can be known for supporting good journalism in the years to come. How might we love local and national reporters as ourselves, even those who seem bent on ignoring all the good things done in the name of Christ? What virtues can Christian scholars in the twenty-first century learn from our journalist neighbors?

We might not readily see it, but journalists and scholars share more in common than we think. Most centrally, the heartbeat of

---

[16]Charissa Koh, Elizabeth Rieth, and Isaiah Johnson, "Papered Over," *World Magazine*, August 16, 2018, https://world.wng.org/2018/08/papered_over.

both vocations is curiosity. At their best, journalists and scholars love learning for its own sake—not to create a salacious headline on one hand, or to receive grant funding on the other, but simply to learn about the beauty and complexity of God's world for the wild and mysterious thing that it is. The word *curious* shares a linguistic root with the word *care*. The connection here is multilayered; curious people care enough about the world to learn about it. But they also use their gleaned knowledge to care for others.

According to the American Press Institute, reflecting on veteran journalists Bill Kovach and Tom Rosenstiel's book *The Elements of Journalism*, journalists possess "an independence of spirit and an open-mindedness and intellectual curiosity that helps the journalist see beyond his or her own class or economic status, race, ethnicity, religion, gender or ego."[17] In this way, curiosity often inspires empathy—to seek to understand what life is like for someone whose context is different from one's own. Journalists remind a community of scholars that learning is above all an act of worship, an exercise in understanding the creation so that the Creator might be more fully praised for his endless creativity.

Second, good journalists and academics possess the virtue of intellectual humility, which is to admit mistakes and the limits of our knowledge even as we eagerly and faithfully pursue the truth. One misconception about journalists is that they promise to be objective—that they promise to give us a full, complete account of reality. This is humanly impossible; a subjective self is always in the mix. Rather, what journalists promise, if they are doing their job, is to use an objective *method* of testing information—what the American Press Institute calls "a transparent approach to evidence—precisely so that

---

[17]"The Elements of Journalism," American Press Institute, accessed October 31, 2019, www .americanpressinstitute.org/journalism-essentials/what-is-journalism/elements-journalism.

personal and cultural biases would not undermine the accuracy of the work."[18]

As a result, good journalists rely on good editors, outside sources, and the standard practices of verification to keep their biases at bay. Likewise, good scholars recognize the limits of their knowledge and blind spots created by race, class, gender, theology, denominational ties, and sometimes by what was eaten for breakfast that morning. They seek to break down siloed departments across campus and look for opportunities to collaborate across disciplines. When they get something wrong, they are quick to admit it, even if it is pointed out by an eighteen-year-old whippersnapper. As Paul reminds tells, "Knowledge puffs up while love builds up" (1 Corinthians 8:1 NIV). Intellectually humble scholars check to ensure they are not getting puffed up on knowledge unmoored from the anchor of love.

Finally, the virtue of service will never lead us astray. Good journalists serve the public by providing information that helps citizens make informed decisions. The late historian Christopher Lasch urged us to "defend democracy not as the most efficient but as the most educational form of government, one that extends the circle of debate as widely as possible and thus forces all citizens to articulate their views, to put their views at risk, and to cultivate the virtues of eloquence, clarity of thought and expression, and sound judgment."[19] The education needed to participate in democracy often comes from journalists who see readers not as passive consumers of entertainment but as crucial members of society whose views deserve to be heard. For every listicle and talking head, there are hundreds of local reporters who work to serve the public, day in and day out.

---

[18]"Elements of Journalism."

[19]Christopher Lasch, *The Revolt of the Elites and the Betrayal of Democracy* (New York: W. W. Norton, 1991), 171.

They put in long hours and face constant criticism; many of them have to report on tragedy, violence, crime, and coverup. As one internet meme goes: "Journalism: It's a tough job with insane hours and pretty crappy pay. On the other hand, everybody hates you."

Twentieth-century humorist Finley Peter Dunne famously said that a newspaper "comforts the afflicted [and] afflicts the comfortable."[20] This chiasmus sounds downright biblical: that when justice and peace reign under the rule of Christ, the poor will be rich and the rich will be poor, the downtrodden will be lifted up and the rulers will be humbled, those who are afflicted in this life will be comforted and those who are comfortable in this life will be afflicted. We get hints of this upside-down kingdom whenever journalists pursue the truth, cast light on dark deeds, and speak for those who cannot speak for themselves. May we more readily welcome the holy affliction of good reporting, knowing that so often the truth stings, but it also heals.

---

[20]David Shedden, "Today in Media History: Mr. Dooley: 'The Job of the Newspaper Is to Comfort the Afflicted and Afflict the Comfortable,'" Poynter, October 7, 2014, www.poynter.org/reporting-editing/2014/today-in-media-history-mr-dooley-the-job-of-the-newspaper-is-to-comfort-the-afflicted-and-afflict-the-comfortable.

Part 3

Personal
Reflection

6

How Reconciliation Saved
My Scholarship

Emmanuel Katongole

When I was approached about being part of this project, I was curious why I was asked, an African Catholic priest in a book directed mostly to American evangelical Christians. What did they want me to say?

I was persuaded by scholarly interests, considering that my efforts in bridging different audiences (Catholic, mainline Protestant, evangelical/academic, practitioner/institutional, grassroots/United States–Africa) represent the kind of public intellectual engagement the project organizers had in mind. Here I could share my story about what I do, how I go about it, the gifts that keep me going as well as the challenges I meet. I immediately thought of Desmond Tutu's beautiful book, written with Mpho Tutu, his youngest daughter. I thought I would perhaps offer a similar reflection as the Tutus do in *Made for Goodness.*[1]

I wish to dedicate this chapter to my friend Chris Rice, without whom the story I tell here would not be possible. Chris's friendship and influence on me during our time and work together at Duke and after is yet another confirmation of God's unexpected and undeserved gifts.
[1]Desmond Tutu and Mpho Tutu, *Made for Goodness and Why This Makes All the Difference* (New York: HarperCollins, 2010).

Of course, for me to think, let alone suggest, that I am doing a similar thing here as Tutu does in his book sounds preposterous. Tutu is not only a highly celebrated individual but also a Nobel laureate whose accomplishments—as archbishop of Cape Town, fierce antiapartheid activist, and former chairperson of the Truth and Reconciliation Commission in South Africa—make him a unique and extraordinary leader. Nevertheless, I find *Made in Goodness* particularly evocative in that in this book Tutu is giving an account of the hope that shapes his life and drives his engagement in the world. Christian life is a life of hope, and the Christian must at all times heed Peter's exhortation to "be prepared to give an answer . . . for the hope that you have," and to do so "with gentleness and respect" (1 Peter 3:15 NIV). That is exactly what Tutu is doing. In the preface to *Made for Goodness*, Tutu notes that he speaks to audiences across the world, and he often gets the same questions:

> Why are you so joyful? How do you keep your faith in people when you see much injustice, oppression, and cruelty? What makes you certain that the world is going to get better? What the questions really want to know is, what do I see that they're missing? How do I see the world and my role in it? How do I see God? What is the faith that drives me? What are spiritual practices that uphold me? What do I see in the heart of humanity and in the sweep of history that confirms my conviction that goodness will triumph?

The answers to these and similar questions lie in the story of divine goodness, within which Tutu locates his life and engagement in the world. "We are made for goodness by God, who is goodness itself. We are all made for and like God."[2] According to Tutu, discovering

---

[2]Tutu, *Made for Goodness*, ix, 8.

that story makes all the difference not only in the way one sees the world, oneself, and others, but also in the way one lives.

First, Tutu notes that when we see "that we are all designed for goodness, and when we recognize that truth," we are able to see the world in a new way, in the way that God does. Second, when we accept that "we are perfectly loved with a love that requires nothing of us, we can stop 'being good' and live into the goodness that is our essence." Third, for Tutu, the story of divine goodness is at the same time "an invitation to wholeness that leads to flourishing for all of us." Equally important for Tutu is how the story of divine goodness shapes practices, what Tutu describes as "disciplines of goodness," such as attentiveness, prayer, savoring, thinking, enjoying and being thankful, rest, forgiveness—disciplines that shape Tutu's spiritual life, daily rhythm, and his leadership and activism, including his fierce advocacy with and on behalf of the oppressed.[3]

My goal in this chapter is to provide a similar account of the story that shapes my scholarship and drives my engagement as a priest, scholar, and practitioner. Before doing so, however, it is important to note that the surprise at the heart of my story points to a reality beyond any particular engagement I might be involved in at any particular time. It is this *beyond* that I want to reflect on and the ways in which it has translated into public scholarly engagement.

A Surprising Journey

I currently serve as professor of theology and peace studies at the University of Notre Dame. As a professor, I have written a number of books. I have also been involved in and helped to found and lead a number of initiatives, including the Center for Reconciliation at Duke Divinity School, Duke Divinity's African Great Lakes Initiative,

---

[3]Tutu, *Made for Goodness*, x, 92.

Share the Blessings, the Bethany House in Entebbe, and, more recently, the Bethany Land Institute.[4] Four years ago, a research assistant pressed me with a question: "Father Emmanuel, you are involved in a number of initiatives and programs. What is the best way to describe you?" I responded by describing myself as a priest, professor, and pilgrim.[5] Looking back, I realize that while the triple designation helped to organize the different commitments around three identities, it did not offer a good sense of the surprise and journey that has been a key dimension of my life. For how does someone born and raised in Uganda, a Catholic priest ordained for the archdiocese of Kampala, end up living and working in the United States? How does a little boy from a small village in Uganda (Malube) end up working under the Magisterial Dome of Our Lady's University? Not only that, but what are the chances that someone who grows up in a house without books ends up obtaining a PhD from one of the top universities in Europe and writing many books?

In a previous publication, I reflected on the journey that took me from Malube to Duke and the many journeys back and forth.[6] Even that essay did not fully capture this sense of surprise. For I often think about my extraordinary journey in terms of *miracle*, and, as I often joke with friends, a veritable proof of God's existence to be added to Thomas Aquinas's five proofs. Behind the joke, however, lies a simple but profound realization, namely, that my life is part of

[4]See "About Us," Center for Reconciliation, accessed March 25, 2020, https://divinity.duke
.edu/initiatives/cfr/about; "African Great Lakes Initiative," Center for Reconciliation, accessed
March 25, 2020, https://divinity.duke.edu/initiatives/cfr/gli; Share the Blessings: Clean Water
and Education Non-profit (website), accessed March 25, 2020, www.share-the-blessings
.org; Bethany House (website), accessed March 25, 2020, www.bethanyhousecentre.com;
Bethany Land Institute (website), accessed March 25, 2020, https://bethanylandinstitute.org.
[5]See Fr. Emmanuel Katongole (website), accessed March 25, 2020, http://emmanuelkatongole
.com.
[6]See Emmanuel Katongole, "A Tale of Many Stories," in *Shaping a Global Theological Mind*,
ed. Darren C. Marks (Burlington, VT: Ashgate, 2008), 89-94.

something bigger; I am caught up in a drama not of my own making, whose final realization lies beyond me. In this way, I feel much the same as a female leader in the civil rights movement who is quoted as repeatedly saying, "I do not know what God is doing, but I am glad to be part of it."

But what is the *it* that I am part of? How has it shaped my understanding of what I am doing as a scholar, as a priest, and as a practitioner? What kind of disciplines does it shape? How have these disciplines helped me to bridge the worlds of my work in the United States and my work in Africa, the concerns of the academy and the concerns of the broader world beyond the academy? Reflecting on this story and the gifts or disciplines it has unleashed or helped to shape in my case will, I trust, invite others to share about the convictions that drive their scholarship as a form of public engagement. My assumption of course is that every Christian scholar, the theologian in particular, is, or at least ought to be, a public intellectual.

The Gift of Reconciliation and the Reconciliation of Fragments

I titled my chapter "How Reconciliation Saved My Scholarship" for the simple reason that the gifts on which I want to reflect are connected to the story of God's reconciling love in the world. I discovered this story in 2005 in the context of my work as founding codirector of the Duke Center for Reconciliation.[7] This is when I was, so to say, born again, again!

Prior to 2005, my scholarship remained largely theoretical, which is to say academic in the narrow sense. Coming out of a philosophical

---

[7]For more on that story, see Emmanuel Katongole and Chris Rice, *Reconciling All Things: A Christian Vision for Justice, Peace, and Healing* (Downers Grove, IL: InterVarsity Press, 2008), 11-20; Katongole, *The Journey of Reconciliation: Groaning for a New Creation in Africa* (Maryknoll, NY: Orbis Books, 2017), ix-xxvi.

background with a PhD in philosophy from Leuven, I investigated Africa's social history and the predictable patterns of violence, poverty, and political instability. I pointed to (1) the need for interruption and alternatives to this social history, and to (2) the role that Christianity in general and the church in particular can play in this effort. However, I did not have a clear sense of the big picture or the telos (i.e., end) of that much-needed interruption. Neither did I offer any concrete examples of the kind of alternative I was calling for. As a result, my scholarship and writing remained abstract and philosophical.

I remember giving a copy of my first book to a former colleague at the major seminary in Uganda. He started reading it immediately that evening. The following morning, he told me he could not get beyond the first chapter, because he found both its language and argument inaccessible. He jokingly asked whether I meant the book to be read. Perhaps part of the problem was the book was the revised and published version of my dissertation, *Beyond Universal Reason*.[8]

While I felt the challenge in my friend's question, I did not know how to write differently. This changed following the invitation in the fall of 2004 by the dean of Duke Divinity School, L. Gregory Jones, to work with Chris Rice to found and codirect a Center for Reconciliation at Duke Divinity School. The invitation marked a major turning point for my life and scholarship; it forced me to get off my philosophical and theoretical horse and attend to the concrete and everyday reality of communities and individuals seeking to live out the gift of God's reconciliation in specific local places. More specifically, the invitation to found and codirect the Center for Reconciliation offered five major but interrelated gifts that continue to shape my scholarship and engagement in its theological, contextual, and practical

---

[8]Emmanuel Katongole, *Beyond Universal Reason: The Relation Between Ethics and Religion in the Work of Stanley Hauerwas* (Notre Dame, IN: University of Notre Dame Press, 2000).

dimensions. By briefly reflecting on these gifts, I will show why and how discovering the story of God's reconciliation has made all the difference. This applies not only to how I view the world but also to how I understand my calling as a priest, a professor, and a pilgrim.

The big picture. As Chris and I worked to establish the vision and mission of the Center for Reconciliation, one of my most profound discoveries was that reconciliation is not so much a process, technique, or event, but a story—the story of God's ongoing journey with creation. This insight might sound self-evident now, but as Chris and I surveyed the landscape of reconciliation programs and ministries, we encountered the expectation and pressure to come up with clear guidelines regarding the stages or skills on "how to" reconcile. As one leader challenged us, "The fire is out there raging. What we need is water to put it out."

We had to resist this pressure for skills and techniques, for, in turning to Scripture, we discovered that reconciliation is first and foremost God's gift. "God was reconciling the world to himself," Paul writes to the Corinthians (2 Corinthians 5:19 NIV).

Discovering reconciliation as the story of God's ongoing journey with creation was therapeutic in a number of ways. First, it allowed me to see how all human endeavors, including scholarship, are part of this drama of reconciliation as God's gift ("All this is from God" [2 Corinthians 5:18 NIV]) and an invitation (God is "making his appeal through us" [2 Corinthians 5:20 NIV]). In this connection, I found particularly helpful and powerful Sam Wells's description of Scripture as a story—a drama that unfolds in five acts: (1) creation, (2) election of people: the story of Israel, (3) the incarnation, (4) the church, and (5) eschaton.[9] In this five-point drama, the Christ event

---

[9]Samuel Wells, *Improvisation: The Drama of Christian Ethics* (Grand Rapids: Brazos, 2004), esp. 53-57.

(incarnation) is the central act, in which God's reconciliation has already been realized: "through Christ," as Paul notes in 2 Corinthians 5:18 (NIV). Moreover, that we now find ourselves in act four of the drama means that the church lives and ministers in that intermediary stage, in the already and not yet, as the story moves to the full realization of God's reconciliation (in the eschaton).[10]

At any rate, the story of reconciliation helped to clarify the goal, the end, the "toward what" of my scholarship. My scholarship would make sense only if it either contributed to or made explicit the story of God's reconciling love in the world. But the fact that reconciliation was God's mission meant that I did not have to take myself or my scholarship too seriously. My efforts were only a tiny subplot in the big story: "the magnificent enterprise" (as Oscar Romero calls it) of God's reconciling work in the world, whose final realization always lies far beyond any one of us.[11]

On another level, however, while discovering the big story of God's reconciling love clarified the goal of my scholarship and also gave it a sense of urgency, it made my life in the academy more complicated. Previously, I understood myself as a scholar who was committed to the pursuit of knowledge. Being a philosopher allowed me a certain measure of neutrality, as well as distance, from my scholarly investigation. Now it was clear that I was no longer neutral; I was committed to a particular type of scholarship, one that illumined God's reconciliation. If previously I had understood myself

---

[10]I have also found the work of another colleague, Richard Hays, *The Moral Vision of the New Testament* (San Francisco: HarperSanFrancisco, 1996), to be quite helpful. In this very influential study, Hays shows a unified ethical vision in the New Testament, centered in the themes of community, cross, and new creation. These are held together by the underlying story of God's reconciling action in the world that has come to a definite fulfillment in the Christ event.

[11]See "A Step Along the Way," a prayer attributed to Oscar Romero, accessed March 25, 2020, www.usccb.org/prayer-and-worship/prayers-and-devotions/prayers/prophets-of-a-future-not-our-own.cfm.

as a philosopher whose work had theological implications, reconciliation was forcing me to become a theologian, and a particular kind of theologian at that.

The kind of scholarship that I was now doing did not fit neatly in the usual category of academic theology. What made it possible was not only my background in theology (having studied theology in the seminary and in Leuven for a master of arts in religious studies), but also that I was not on a tenure-track appointment. A year before the invitation to the founding of the center, I had turned down a tenure-track appointment, as my bishop had indicated he needed me back in Uganda within three years. Not being on tenure track gave me the freedom to move between philosophical analysis and theological argumentation, and thus to push and cross the boundaries of standard academic specialization.

A calling. The second gift was a sense of personal calling that involved seeing myself as a bridge. Prior to 2005, prior to discovering the story of reconciliation, I struggled with my identity as an African living in the United States, as a Catholic priest at Methodist Duke, as a philosopher teaching theology and world Christianity. Even though I had learned, following Stanley Hauerwas, to describe myself as "resident alien,"[12] I was internally troubled with a sense of not belonging and of being a misfit. With the discovery of the notion of reconciliation, I began to name my displacement and "exile" in the United States and at Methodist Duke as a gift—part of what it means to be an ambassador of God's reconciliation.

This proved to be a watershed moment for me. I could see and understand my life in North Carolina as a kind of diplomatic posting and see my call as one of bridging worlds that often remained apart.

---

[12]Stanley Hauerwas and William H. Willimon, *Resident Aliens: Life in the Christian Colony,* expanded 25th anniversary ed. (Nashville: Abingdon, 2014).

As Alexander Schmemann notes in his *Journals*: "The tragedy is that each fragment wants to be the whole . . . and passionately denies the others. Each one perceives Christ only through his own experience, his own vision. No one sees his own limitations, his own relative character in Christ." For Schmemann, the truth lies in the unity and synthesis of fragments. "All my fragmented experiences are not due to chance. . . . They force me to come to a synthesis, to overcome the fragmented character, the breaking of pieces." Like Schmemann, I began to see my calling in terms of "trying—and praying— . . . to unite all those fragments and to return them to life in and through Christ." For Schmemann, he *must* do so, because it is the truth; he *can* do so because he "understands these fragments and can identify literally with each of them."[13] I felt the same way.

Born in Uganda, now living in America, of Rwandan parents, one Hutu the other Tutsi, a Catholic at a Protestant seminary—my own identity reflected a coming together of different fragments, which I now began to see as a mirror to what the church is called to be. This is what made particularly disturbing the Rwandan genocide and the fact that Christians killed others in the name of Hutu and Tutsi, suggesting that the blood of tribalism is deeper than the waters of baptism. For as I now understood it, Christian life is an invitation into a new creation, a new we.

Accordingly, in *Mirror to the Church*, I note that the goal of mission is not simply to build on our so-called natural identities, Hutu, Tutsi, African, American, but to form a new social reality—the reality of a

---

[13]Alexander Schmemann, *The Journals of Father Alexander Schmemann 1973-1983* (Crestwood, NY: St. Vladimir's Seminary Press, 2000), 92. I am grateful to Chris Rice, who first drew my attention to Schmemann's *Journals* at our very first retreat following the invitation to establish the Center for Reconciliation. This was early December 2004 at Trinity Center on Emerald Isle, a retreat center that Chris and I visited frequently. Schmemann's *Journals* have been a constant source of inspiration and have offered crucial insights daily as well as at moments of major decisions.

church that "gathers" (Greek *ekklesia*) into one body fragments from all nations, tribes, and languages. Accordingly, I argue, the primary mission of the church is not to make America more Christian, but rather to make American Christians less American, and Rwandan Christians less Rwandan. Christians globally should become part of the new social reality made possible by God's reconciling love in the world.[14] That is, each on its own—America, Rwanda, Hutu, Tutsi, Catholic, Protestant—remains but a fragment; only by coming together do they reflect the reality of God's new creation.

In this connection, I found Andrew Walls's description of the "Ephesian moment" quite helpful. For Walls, the original Ephesian moment was the coming together of Jews and Gentiles for the first time, which Paul celebrates (in the letter to the Ephesians) as the coming together of fragments—those "who once were far away" (Ephesians 2:13 NIV). He notes how it is the coming together that created the new reality of the church and thus revealed Christ's full stature.[15] For Walls, this coming together requires—and here Walls is following Paul—a journey from the "old" (man, Adam, creation) into the "new," what Walls describes as the pilgrim principle.

During this very season of my journey, I began reading Miroslav Volf's *Exclusion and Embrace*. It points to a similar conclusion by highlighting Christian life as a journey. This is what Volf describes

---

[14]Emmanuel Katongole with Jonathan Wilson-Hartgrove, *Mirror to the Church: Resurrecting Faith After Genocide in Rwanda* (Grand Rapids: Zondervan, 2009), 156.

[15]Andrew Walls, "'The Ephesian Moment' at Crossroads in Christian History," in *The Cross-Cultural Process in Christian History* (Maryknoll, NY: Orbis Books, 2002), 72-84. Elsewhere Walls elaborates on the indigenizing and pilgrim principles, both of which are at work within Christian history. "Not only does God in Christ take people as they are: He takes them in order to transform them into what He wants them to be. Along with the indigenizing principle which makes his faith a place to feel at home, the Christian inherits the pilgrim principle, which whispers to him that he has no abiding city and warns him that to be faithful to Christ will put him out of step with his society." See Andrew Walls, "The Gospel as Prisoner and Liberator of Culture," in *The Missionary Movement in Christian History: Studies in the Transmission of Faith* (Maryknoll, NY: Orbis Books, 2004), 8.

as Abrahamic principle. Volf argues that at the very foundation of Christian faith stands the towering figure of Abraham. Before Genesis records that he "believed," it records that he "went" forth (Genesis 15:6; 12:1-4). Christian faith is an invitation into a similar Abrahamic revolution. "To be a child of Abraham and Sarah and to respond to the call of their God means to make an exodus, to start a voyage, become a stranger."[16] Thus, working with the Center for Reconciliation was allowing me to embrace my pilgrim existence as both a gift and an invitation, which could illumine and facilitate the coming together of various fragments (of the world and of the church) in the journey toward God's new creation.

Multiple audiences. The third gift was the gift of multiple audiences and of coming to see my scholarship as one of "translation." As Chris and I worked together on the vision of the center, we invited different groups—scholars, students, and practitioners—to help us shape the center's vision. Simultaneously, we traveled to acquaint ourselves with the different reconciliation ministries working in different places of brokenness: Voice of Calvary in Mississippi; New Song in Sandtown, Baltimore; Religious Coalition for a Nonviolent Durham, North Carolina; Word Made Flesh in Omaha; and in East Africa, the Mennonite Central Committee, World Vision International, and African Leadership and Reconciliation Ministries, among others.

My first visit to the annual Christian Community Development Association conference in Indianapolis opened my eyes even wider. The vibrant gathering of practitioners from around the United States surprised me. I did not imagine the existence of such a rich array of ministries seeking to live out the story of reconciliation in the world.

---

[16]Miroslav Volf, *Exclusion and Embrace: A Christian Exploration of Identity, Otherness, and Reconciliation* (Nashville: Abingdon, 1996), 39.

Chris and I started dreaming of forming a Christian Community Development Association–like gathering in East Africa. We invited Christian leaders of different denominations from different countries of the African Great Lakes region: Uganda, Rwanda, Kenya, Congo, Burundi, Tanzania, and South Sudan. In this region with longstanding suspicion and animosity between countries and denominations, Catholics found themselves sitting next to evangelicals, Congolese next to Rwandans.

The first day was awkward because evangelicals did not know how to talk to, let alone pray with, Catholics (and the other way around); Congolese did not know what to say to Rwandans, whose country had invaded theirs. At the end of three days, it was gratifying to see not only how many diverse groups overcame some of their fears but new friendships emerge across the divides.

At the fourth Gathering of the Great Lakes Initiative, as we called these annual meetings, one visiting leader from the Mennonite Central Committee office in Kenya remarked: "This is the most dynamic, spirit-filled ecumenical gathering I have encountered during my five years in East Africa." Perhaps his most significant observation was that "the primary goal of the gathering is not to reconcile Catholics, mainline Protestants and Evangelicals. But by focusing on the story of God's reconciling love in the world, we find out divisions and our differences as Catholics, Protestants and Evangelicals to be less interesting."[17] We also sought to bridge the gap between the academy and the broader world. I did not know that something like a Christian Community Development Association existed. This confirmed how the world of practitioners is often invisible to the academy, just as the world of practitioners often remains locked up

---

[17]Personal conversation with Mennonite Central Committee regional representatives, Bujumbura, Burundi, January 10, 2010.

in its own false sense of self-sufficiency. At one gathering of Christian activists, the speaker said something to the effect that "the good thing is that here there are no theologians!"

Our goal was to connect these worlds. We started sending Duke master of divinity students on field education to what we called teaching communities, and we invited practitioners into the academy (Teaching Communities Week, Summer Institute). Then we envisioned literature that would speak to both theologians and practitioners. This is how we founded the Resources for Reconciliation book series (published in partnership with InterVarsity Press), pairing a practitioner and a theologian to write each book. Chris's and my book *Reconciling All Things* was the lead title, with six other books emerging out of that project. Now in its eighth edition and fourth translation, *Reconciling All Things* struck a chord among many readers because of its deep theological message presented in a simple and accessible manner.

Working with various audiences was forcing me to learn to write in a simple, straightforward way to reach as broad an audience as possible. Translating the thick theological jargon of the academy into graspable concepts resonated with readers, along with connecting the rich stories of the practitioners to theoretical frameworks and speculative notions of the academy, as Hauerwas has emphasized.[18] The overwhelming positive response to *Reconciling All Things*, and to *Mirror to the Church*—both written in simple straightforward manner for a broader audience—confirmed the hunger for good but accessible theological literature.

This experience and the establishment of the center prompted the rewrite of *The Sacrifice of Africa*, which was then already accepted

---

[18]Hauerwas describes this as the discipline of "writing-out." To write-out, he notes, "is to write in a fashion that welcomes the reader who may not share our academic specialty but who nonetheless may identify and resonate with the issue or problem that the article addresses." See Stanley Hauerwas, "'Writing-In' and 'Writing-Out,'" *Modern Theology* 26, no. 1 (2010): 61-66.

for publication.[19] Doing so meant not only attending to the style of writing but also shaping its argument around stories—which was another significant gift related to the discovery of reconciliation.

Stories. Hauerwas's narrative theology continued to engage me.[20] Working with the notion of reconciliation further led me to appreciate more personally how stories are at the heart of the theological project. In other words, with the notion of reconciliation, my work took on a distinctly narrative character. This led me to the conclusion that the theologian is first and foremost a storyteller, though not in a facile way of telling stories as anecdotes.

There are significant methodological, epistemological, and practical implications connected to story in general. First, in terms of methodology, I have come to recognize that an adequate conversation about reconciliation needs to bring together three moments of inquiry: theological, contextual, and practical knowledge. Each of these moments revolves around *story*: with the story of God and stories of Scripture driving the theological moment, the stories of the politics and economics of places driving the contextual moment, and the stories of individuals and communities driving the practical moment of reflection.

Connected with this observation is an epistemological claim, that the nature and structure of reality is revealed through stories. Accordingly, the very point of the gift of new creation within which the story of reconciliation operates is to invite Christians into a distinct epistemology, which is to say a distinct way of seeing or knowing reality. But since the truth of this distinct way cannot be known apart from the lives of the individuals and communities it shapes, stories

---

[19]Emmanuel Katongole, *The Sacrifice of Africa: A Political Theology for Africa* (Grand Rapids: Eerdmans, 2010).

[20]See Katongole, *Beyond Universal Reason.* See also Emmanuel Katongole, "Hauerwasian Hooks, Stories and the Social Imagination of the 'Next Christendom,'" in *A Future for Africa: Critical Essays in Christian Social Imagination* (Eugene, OR: Wipf & Stock, 2017), 231-52.

provide both the argument and evidence. The combined effect of all this is to make narrative and story central to my work.

More recently, I have come to describe what I do as theological portraiture. This reflects the nomenclature from Sara Lawrence-Lightfoot. She describes portraiture as a form of inquiry that blends "aesthetics and empiricism in an effort to capture the complexity, dynamics, and subtlety of human experience and organizational life."[21] Lightfoot also describes the portraitist as a storyteller—a unique storyteller who is interested not only in producing complex, subtle description in context, but also in searching for the central story, developing a convincing and authentic narrative.

The portraitist is not simply listening to stories; she is "*listening for a story*."[22] This depiction of the portraitist is particularly helpful in understanding what one's scholarship is about—including mine. I am listening for the story of God's reconciling love in the world and seeking to understand and display how this story is either resisted (by structures, systems, communities, and individuals) or embraced. My overall goal is to portray what embracing the gift of God's reconciliation concretely looks like and, concomitantly, what is hopeful or salvific about this story particularly in the context of Africa's social history.

Another reason I like Lawrence-Lightfoot's notion of portraiture is its emphasis on audience. The portraitist seeks to speak to a broad and diverse audience and is driven by an explicit activist impulse for intervention and community building. She notes, "The attempt is to move beyond the academy's inner circle, to speak in a language that

---

[21]Sara Lawrence-Lightfoot and Jessica Hoffmann Davis, *The Art and Science of Portraiture* (San Francisco: John Wiley, 1997), xv. See Emmanuel Katongole, *Born from Lament* (Grand Rapids: Eerdmans, 2017), 33-38.

[22]Fenwick D. English, "A Critical Appraisal of Sara Lawrence-Lightfoot's *Portraiture* as a Method of Educational Research," *Educational Researcher* (October 1, 2000): 22, http://edr .sagepub.com/content/29/7/21.full.pdf.

is not coded or exclusive, and to develop texts that will seduce the readers into thinking more deeply about issues that concern them. Portraitists write to inform and inspire readers."[23]

Hope. Reconciliation is a journey of hope. More specifically, it is about learning to see that, even in the midst of violence and hatred, God is always sowing seeds of hope. Isaiah's message to a beleaguered, exiled, and disheartened people is true today. "See, I am doing a new thing! / Now it springs up; do you not perceive it? / I am making a way in the wilderness" (Isaiah 43:19 NIV).

The journey of reconciliation is in great part about learning to see and receive those unexpected gifts of hope. It is also about learning to name and thus tell where and how those unexpected gifts are happening. Thus, Peter's exhortation to Christians who, not unlike the community of Isaiah, were experiencing a sense of exile and hostility to "always be prepared to give an answer to everyone who asks you to give the reason for the hope that you have"—and to do so with gentleness and humility (1 Peter 3:15 NIV). In the end, this is what my scholarship is about: seeing, naming, and telling hope.

My attempt to live into the disciplines of seeing, naming, and telling hope has taken two distinct but overlapping trajectories: a critical and constructive direction. The critical direction has been focused around the question of what's going on, especially in Africa—seeking to understand and make sense (or make thinkable) the recurrent challenges of poverty, violence, and political instability in Africa. All of this in a continent incredibly rich and full of so much potential.

In this attempt, I engage various scholars, social scientists, philosophers, and theologians while researching the wound at the heart of Africa's social history, seeking to connect that with the wound in

---

[23]Lawrence-Lightfoot and Davis, *Art and Science of Portraiture*, 10. See also Katongole, *Born from Lament*, 33-38.

God's own heart. German Reformed theologian Jürgen Moltmann is right: "Theology comes from the passion of God, the open wound in one's life, from Job's indictment of God and the accusing cry of the Crucified Christ to God's wrath, from the absence of God, and experiences of the suffering of this present time."[24] To this effect, lament has been a central theme of my scholarship, as it is at the heart of any vision and praxis of hope.[25]

The constructive direction of seeing and naming hope has resulted in a number of practical engagements, the overall goal of which is to nurture and shape the praxis and experience of hope. What is perhaps remarkable about the various practical engagements is the sense of journey, how one thing has led to another. For a number of years, I have led journeys to Uganda and Rwanda, which I call Pilgrimages of Pain and Hope.[26] I invite on these pilgrimages my students, colleagues, parishioners, and friends from around the world to come and see Africa. I am, of course, aware that Africa is not so much a place as a concept.[27] Therefore, during the pilgrimages of pain and hope, I take the pilgrims to particular places with the hope that that they may know Africa differently and become affectionate with the places and people they visit.

Out of one such pilgrimage emerged Share the Blessings, a not-for-profit organization that supports education and water needs in Uganda. In 2006, Chris Rice and I invited a group of Christian leaders from the Africa Great Lakes region (see above), shared with them a theological vision of reconciliation, and offered them an opportunity

---

[24]See Jürgen Moltmann, "A Lived Theology," in Marks, ed., *Shaping a Theological Mind*, 94.
[25]See most recently Katongole, *Born from Lament*.
[26]See Emmanuel Katongole, "Mission and the Ephesian Moment of World Christianity: Pilgrimages of Pain and Hope and the Economics of Eating Together," *Mission Studies* 29 (2012): 183-200.
[27]See my forthcoming *Who Are My People: The Invention of Love in Sub-Saharan Africa*.

to share their stories of pain and hope in the journey of reconciliation. That initiative has turned into an annual Institute for Christian Reconciliation gathering that draws more than 150 leaders from East Africa and beyond. For a week the participants at the institute learn and share their stories and experience of reconciliation.

The need for a place of rest and renewal for the Christian leaders in reconciliation prompted me to found Bethany House in Entebbe. This is a retreat center serving practitioners in the region.[28] More recently, I also cofounded the Bethany Land Institute, through which I work with young people in the rural diocese of Luweero to address the challenges of food insecurity, deforestation, and poverty in rural communities.

In all these initiatives, I am trying to accomplish three things. First, I am pursuing a vision of reconciliation, which, as Fred Bahnson and Norman Wirzba remind us, is always connected to a place: "Rather than being simply the absence of violence, reconciliation takes us to a physical place—a plot of land—that puts down roots, produces food, provides stability and hospitality, fosters healthy relationships and inspires joy. Shalom presupposes people living securely in the land, which means that land and people together are being respected and nurtured."[29]

Second, I am seeking to bridge the theoretical and the practical aspects of my scholarship in ways that advance the theory and praxis of reconciliation. In this connection, Congolese theologian Kä Mana's observations are both an indictment and an invitation. "The goal of African theology and Christianity," Kä Mana writes, "must be to transform Africa rather than just explain it; to change it

---

[28]For a more extended reflection on the story of Bethany House and the theology that underlies it, see Emmanuel Katongole, *Stories from Bethany: On the Faces of the Church in Africa* (Nairobi: Paulines, 2012).

[29]Fred Bahnson and Norman Wirzba, *Making Peace with the Land: God's Call to Reconcile with Creation* (Downers Grove, IL: InterVarsity Press, 2012), 66.

positively rather than just study it; to create history rather than just to interpret it."[30] My way of saying this is that the task is to reflect, extend, and make evident the hope of God's reconciling love in the world, which requires both theoretical and practical engagement.

Third is the discipline of seeing, naming, and telling hope, which involves the very praxis of hope. Hope is not a thing but an experience and a practice. Accordingly, seeing hope involves a particular form of knowledge—knowledge that involves practice; knowledge that comes from and with the very practice of hope. This knowledge is local and concrete. For, as Wendell Berry notes, thinking and acting locally is what "keeps work within the reach of love."[31] This is what makes the very practice of seeing and naming hope a form of affection and caretaking. As such, it is not merely about what it is able to do for others as what it is able to cultivate within one's own life: one's own ability to live (with hope) within the sluggish between of the already and the not yet of God's reconciling love.

Berry's many years of environmental restoration and activism led him to a conclusion, namely that the real work of saving the planet is small, humble, and humbling, and yet, insofar as it involves love, pleasing and rewarding. How much that observation is true about hope, and how there seems to be no way of discovering that apart from participation in an activity that advances hope for others as well as within oneself.

For the Life of the World

I am sure many are wondering where my reflection is headed. I am supposed to explore the habits necessary for public intellectuals to

---

[30]Cited in Kalemba Mwanbazambi, "Kä Mana: Champion of the Theology of Reconstruction," in *African Theology: The Contribution of the Pioneers*, ed. Benezet Bujo (Nairobi: Paulines, 2012), 154.
[31]Wendell Berry, "Out of Your Car, Off Your Horse," *Atlantic*, February 1991, www.theatlantic .com/magazine/archive/1991/02/out-your-car-your-horse/309159.

make the complex matters yielded by the academy accessible to a wider array of learned communities. Instead, I have just offered snippets from my own story.

While these snippets might be helpful to get a sense of what I am trying to get at in my work, they do not offer a full sense of the skills that public intellectuals need. I do not offer those skills, because I do not think that public intellectuals are a special category of scholars (which lets the rest of us off the hook). Rather, are not all Christian scholars public intellectuals? Is not their scholarship, indeed their engagement, supposed to advance the kingdom of God and the common good?

My goal in reflecting on the gifts I discovered within the context of founding and codirecting a center for reconciliation at a major research university, and how these gifts continue to shape my scholarship and engagement in the world, is to invite other Christian scholars to reflect on their work and what it is they are trying to accomplish through their scholarship. By way of conclusion, it might be helpful to point to one concern that often arises in relation to scholarship pursued from a distinctly Christian point of view, namely, its assumed narrow base. Doing so will help to make explicit the vision of the church—the context of my work.

My assumption is that the role of the Christian scholar is connected to the knowledge and experience of God—in this case, God's reconciling love in the world. But that knowledge is very particular in that it is connected to the life, death, and resurrection of Christ and to the claim that God's reconciling love in the world has come to a definite realization in Christ. Such a claim cannot but strike many as too confessional and too small in an increasingly secular and pluralistic world and in the academy, which is supposed to remain neutral so as to appeal to as many audiences as possible. Doesn't scholarship grounded within a Christian vision instead of promoting the common good (in which also non-Christians participate) simply limit one's audience and in the end encourage Christians into a sectarian mentality? My simple answer is no.

Far from constricting the Christian scholar's audience, a Christian vision expands it exponentially. Let me explain by reflecting on a question a graduate student from China raised in a seminar. We had read *Reconciling All Things*. In the discussion, the student noted how he liked and sympathized with a number of sentiments in the book, but he found its focus as reflected in its subtitle, *A Christian Vision of Reconciliation*, to be "too small." The student found this to be ironic in a book that claims that God reconciles all things. Instead of offering "a Christian vision of reconciliation," he wondered, should the authors be offering instead a vision of reconciliation that includes everyone?

I responded by noting that a Christian vision of reconciliation does indeed include everyone, but how do we get to that everyone? I made reference to three temptations (identified by Sam Wells) that must be avoided in thinking about the church as the body of Christ in the world.[32] The first temptation is to make the world or society the principal location of Christian ethics. Simply put, this temptation assumes that since God's love is for everyone, there is nothing distinctive about Christian convictions. What Christians believe is what everyone believes, even though they might use different language. The task for the Christian scholar is to find that common ground by translating Christian convictions in a manner and language that appeals to everyone. This temptation, which is closely associated with what John Milbank describes as the posture of "false humility," ends up, according to Wells, making the church invisible.[33]

---

[32]Wells, *Improvisation*, 39-40.
[33]The pathos of modern theology, Milbank notes, "is its false humility." By this Milbank means that theology has allowed its "social contribution" to be shaped by the secular disciplines of political theory, economics, and sociology. That this is the case has been due to the

The second temptation is to assume that because the church is the key location of theology, God's primary way of working in the world is the church, and God has no purpose for the rest of creation. The temptation often results in a certain sectarian posture that assumes that God works primarily in and exclusively within the church. In relation to reconciliation, this assumes the vision of God's reconciliation is simply "for us" who have accepted Christ. This temptation, according to Wells, succeeds in making the world invisible.

The third temptation, which Wells also describes as a form of gnosticism, is to assume that the location of theology is in the heart and mind of the individual Christian. This temptation finally turns Christian faith into a form of personal piety, whose goal is the close personal relationship between the Christian and God. This temptation, according to Wells, makes the church captive within a *spiritual* realm of doctrinal purity and devotional piety. Thus, "Christians may engage in the most damaging public practices while still assuming that thinking 'the right things' about salvation or having 'a close personal relationship' with God ensures that righteousness remains with them."[34]

I drew attention to the three temptations for two closely connected reasons. First is to highlight that God's gift of reconciliation is for the world—not merely for Christians. However, for that gift to be truly for the world requires the church as community to have a fuller understanding of the gift itself. In the end, they need to see themselves as ambassadors of God's reconciling love in the world.

The irony, therefore, is that the more grounded one is in the story of God's reconciling love, which is connected to the life, death, and resurrection of Christ, the more one appreciates that this is not

---

assumption that there is a social reality that exists independently from any particular, historical vision of human life. See John Milbank, *Theology and Social Theory: Beyond Secular Reason*, Signposts in Theology (Malden, MA: Blackwell, 1990), 1.

[34]Wells, *Improvisation*, 40.

simply about "us" or about our small or big church, but about the whole world. Yet that conviction is itself shaped by and through particular communities and practices. It is through these practices that Christians are introduced to, initiated into, and formed in the story of God's reconciling love, which has been realized in Christ. Far from absolving Christians from engaging the outside world, the fact that God has reconciled the world in Christ deepens, intensifies, and explodes that engagement beyond church walls, however defined.

Second is to highlight how a Christian vision of reconciliation points to a particular vision of the church as the body of Christ. The church remains distinct not by separating itself from the world but by losing itself into the world—for the life of the world. Pope Francis evokes this sense of church as action when he refers to the church as a field hospital. The church's unique location and mission, Pope Francis states, is at the "frontiers," where she enacts the social process of healing—the healing of all sorts of wounds. In this action, the pope tells us, the church reveals what it means to be human. It encompasses our shared identity as created in God's image. It initiates new historical processes and social possibilities that reflect God's compassion in the world.[35] In this way, the church becomes at once the midwife, agent, and demonstration of the revolution—a revolution of tenderness, of God's reconciling love in the world. This is the kind of ecclesiology that underpins and drives my scholarship and engagement in the world as a priest, professor, and pilgrim.

---

[35]Antonio Spadaro, SJ, "A Big Heart Open to God: Interview with Pope Francis," *America*, September 30, 2013, www.americamagazine.org/faith/2013/09/30/big-heart-open-god-interview -pope-francis.

Concluding Conversation

An Interview with John M. Perkins

David Wright

Wright: Dr. John Perkins is a minister, civil rights activist, a Bible teacher, a best-selling author, philosopher, community developer, a follower of Jesus, and a lover of Scripture—whenever you hear Dr. Perkins speak, his speech is peppered with Scripture. He is the founder and president emeritus of the John and Vera Mae Perkins Foundation for Justice, Reconciliation & Community Development with his wife, Vera Mae Perkins. In 2019, Wesley Seminary at Indiana Wesleyan University established the John and Vera Mae Perkins Collaborator with Christ Award on behalf of John and Vera Mae, which is awarded to men and women who serve together in the life of the church, based on the example that Dr. Perkins and Vera Mae have shown us over the years of successful ministry. He's the cofounder of the Christian Community Development Association—and before that, a very prolific ministry with Voice of Calvary, with Mendenhall Ministries (Mississippi), and with Harambee Ministries in Pasadena. God has used Dr. Perkins to be the generative force in many ministries across our country. He holds more honorary doctorate degrees than I can name here and has authored, I believe, seventeen books, including his latest, *He Calls Me Friend*.[1]

---

[1] John M. Perkins (with Karen Waddles), *He Calls Me Friend: The Healing Power of Friendship in a Lonely World* (Chicago: Moody, 2019).

The work of Dr. Perkins brings the question of what it means to be a public intellectual who is a Christian into the arena of real lives. In Dr. Perkin's speech you hear the passion, the rootedness, and the experience of real people. You hear the drivenness of the cross of Christ, the reality of Jesus in us that doesn't allow us merely to see the struggles of people's lives and walk away. We have to get engaged. The gospel of Christ compels us to be engaged in the life of those around us. This is not just a theoretical exercise. When you watch the ministry that God has given to Dr. Perkins, you see a profound example of engagement with people who are struggling to make sense of life and to enjoy the best that God has created for us.

The topic for this interview is "public intellectuals and the common good—the view from the church." Let's first turn to the view from the church. Dr. Perkins, as you consider your ministry and how God has used you over the years in the church and beyond the church, you no doubt have had some conviction about what the common good means. What is your definition of the common good?

Perkins: Quickly, I would say it would be *human life*. I think that our nation's founding documents affirm that. I think the Bible affirms that. Maybe the best extract of that from the Bible would be "in the image of God he created them" [Genesis 1:27].

And then the intellectual aspect would be that he made humans the subduers and the stewards of life, as stewards of resources planted in the earth. "The earth is the LORD's and the fullness thereof, and all that were therein" [see Psalm 24:1]. So life would be that stewardship. The idea is to know this God, to know that he's love and to make him known. And then to work for him, to worship him, and to serve him—all of that's the one word *stewardship*.

We are stewards of the intellect. He said that when he said to subdue the earth, the animals, all that's in the earth [Genesis 1:28]. We are responsible for managing that. That's why, then, when Jesus acknowledged the poor as those who were disenfranchised and did not get the benefit of it, he started his ministry. "The Spirit of the Lord God Almighty is upon me. He has anointed me to preach the good news" [Luke 4:18]. The good news is that "I've come that they might have life and that they might have it more abundantly" [John 10:10]. The Lord formed the world. God went down to the rock and made justice the foundation of his whole reign.

In eternity, the Lord said something like this: "Lo, I come"—the incarnational thought that Christ is coming is the greatest human thought in history, that God would incarnate himself back in eternity. He said, "Lo, I come." That's what makes that night in Bethlehem so important. It was the longest longing in the history of the world. "Behold, I bring you good news of great joy, which will be for all people, all people, all people. But unto you is born this night in the city of David a Savior, which is Christ the Lord" [Luke 2:10-11].

And so the common good, in the final analysis, would be loving justice, loving justice, if you could get it down to the very core. God through the waters and through the flood. God framed the foundation of life upon justice. We don't understand that. We have allowed our social-economic system to push out justice. I love the thought of capitalism, but all [social] systems need to come out of God's prophetic voice. We might have to be like John the Baptist. That's what God called the church to be. The church was to be salt and light in the world [Matthew 5:13-14]. Light is one of those unending attributes of God; you can't find [an] end in a light, it's so deep. Darkness can't put out light. This would be one of the most fundamental verses in the Bible.

Since we're talking about enlightenment, since we're talking about academics, we're talking about our responsibility as having the gift of subduing society—that's a big responsibility. That's why he gave the earth to us. That word *subdue* meant to look at it, examine it, continue to look at it—and it will provide what humans have need of. God who called the light to shine out of darkness [John 1:5]—that God has shined that light into the academic human community. It's that light of intelligence. And that's why God calls us salt and light. Salt, it's to preserve and continue. Light, it's to keep on looking into it. And so we do have a wonderful stewardship responsibility.

This honors me and energizes me, talking about these things—to build your life on things eternal—this honors me. I long for this kind of dialogue, conversation.

Wright: Your career spans quite a period of time, going back to the civil rights movement in the sixties. How have you seen the public role of Christian leaders change over the years from the civil rights movement in the sixties until today?

Perkins: I think education and voters' rights would have been our greatest achievement. [Previously] education was built on [the reality of] separate and unequal—which developed inferior people. Not only did it not affirm people's dignity, but it "de-firmed" their dignity. That's why racial reconciliation doesn't work. Because we have "niggerized" racism. We have created a word that dehumanizes people.

We have made hate a value. This [last election] was the first election that I saw hate dominate the opposition. [It was] paralyzing. That's a change. We have reprofiled people. We have extended the profile, now, to others outside of blacks. Blacks were the easiest target. Now we've expanded that. Hate was never to be a virtue; hate was never to be used as an advantage. It was always a warning. Hate is the initiative of sin; it is to rebel against God. And now we have made it a value. This is dangerous.

We have got to move toward dignity. That's my life's work. I'm trying to do that now. I've been afraid to [take this direction] at first because what I found over the years in the civil rights movement [was this]: If you tell people too much truth, and they don't implement it, they don't fail; you fail. If you tell people to stop doing something and replace it with what you have, you walk a very thin line. I understood that. So I would never tell [people] to stop. I would tell [them] to add to that, sort of the way the Bible put it, add to [their] knowledge [2 Peter 1:5-8]. [Doing this draws on] the power of responsibility, the power of initiative, the power of human passion that drives people to accomplish things.

To education we can add human dignity. I think of [the example of children's] dolls. Black kids believed that they were inferior; they believed that white dolls were superior. We did that in our racism. We branded white as superior and black as inferior. Then we had a system to guarantee it. It cost a lot of money, a lot of time, a lot of policemen, a lot of jails. In our society, it was a waste. The quickest way forward would be that, in education, we could affirm the human dignity of all. "We hold these truths . . ." I mean that's, a big one. "One nation, under God, with liberty and justice for all."

We've been enfranchised. I'm here. We're talking as equals. That was the idea [of this conference], so we can hear each other and we can learn from each other. A learning environment, where you can think that other folks have dignity. Other folks have something to add. I found that in my Bible study. A newcomer who knew nothing came to my Bible class and asked a question I had never thought of. I don't know whether we as black and white have teamed up enough to use the progress [we've made]. Some of the schools in real black areas are teaming up with white and black small colleges, to bring that relationship that's missing when we miss out on justice.

Justice: we make social justice an issue of the left, and that's a mistake. God's justice is comprehensive. It is social, it is criminal, it is holistic. Justice is justice for all and for all phases [of society]. If we [had tried] to do that it probably would have saved us.

[In 1972] when my civil rights case went to the Fifth Circuit Court, the judge who voted for us wrote 119 pages in our favor. And he was all on it. He said John Perkins is "like Mordecai at the gates" [Esther 2]. His evidence says that he needs to go in. So the struggle has been long but a great thing. Some very discouraged young blacks would say it hasn't changed. Some discouraged young whites will say it hasn't changed. But I'm here!

There have been a lot of changes, but I note especially those for dignity and education, starting with *Brown v. Board of Education.* We make broader rights now, have enfranchised [African Americans] as political actors. President Obama put together the pieces— the discouraged pieces and the ambitious pieces—he put it together first. He was the first person to take the blacks, the educated whites, and the middle class and put them together. We've made a lot of creative progress. And that's what I like about what you guys [the participants at the symposium] are doing. If these principles can be repeated and taught to our students.

Wright: I've heard you talk about the genesis of your entry into ministry and into the public sphere. You've had an enormous impact in many different cities, many societies. Your own experience and influence has spread across the country. What began that journey for you, what thrust you into the public sphere?

Perkins: Memory is powerful. I have asked that question too. I think it was my mother dying when I was seven months old. We were not Christians. We were bootleggers and gamblers, people and family that worked outside of the law. And somehow or another, when they experience justice, it's never justice to them. My mother died of a disease, they call it pellagra. That's the way to define people who died from nutrition deficiency. So my mother died of starvation. I was seven months old living on a plantation, which was a continuation of the slave system. That system wasn't broken until voters' rights had some influence. Voters rights and education brought dignity—in peaceful protests, we put our bodies on the line when our dignity was challenged.

So my grandmother nurtured me in the house. Most of my aunts had babies out of wedlock. We had a big family, without the social enlightenment in that regard. The first thing I can remember was being told, "Your mother's dead." I suspect that I was playing in the house with the other kids, maybe out of control, and one of my caretaking aunts said, "Your mother is dead."

As I look back on it, I think that's critical to my journey: that death, that poverty. And then when I came to know Christ in California—the nurture of both black and white. People were glad I became a Christian. White folk were glad I became a Christian. I've been ministering to white folks and black folks since the first day I became a Christian. [As a new Christian] I thought that's what reconciliation was.

You know, I have never felt humanly inferior. I avoided that by the way I grew up. I grew up on a plantation, and we played ball with the white boys. We make athletics so powerful; you're on a playing field together. It's level. People always say to me, "Jackie Robinson opened the doors for blacks in baseball and athletics." I say, Are you crazy?

He took the fence down. You make him too narrow. He put us on equal footing.

Wright: You came to know Christ in California. When did you know that your ministry was going to have such a public impact?

Perkins: Vera Mae, my wife, came from a religious community. So she would carry the kids to church sometimes. Our son Spencer went to this Good News Club that was sponsored by whites and blacks in the community, and they would get children in particular who didn't go to church. At this club my son heard the truth of the gospel. That story is the power of God. It's more than a human story, so it has its own inspiration of power. He came home singing a song that I heard as the gospel: Jesus loves the little children. All the children of the world. Red, brown, yellow, black, and white, they're all precious in his sight. At that same time, the governor of Arkansas was standing at the door [of the school] to keep nine little black children from coming in.

You don't change society until you change people's religious beliefs. All revolution confronts the religion of the time. Communism had to confront the czar because the priests had become shacklings of the czar. We didn't get change in Mississippi until we confronted Baptist people. Black folks in Louisiana didn't get influence until they confronted the Catholics.

Bad religion—that's what most of the Epistles are about. All but two of the Epistles are about heresy, with the exception of Philippians and probably Philemon. The rest were about heresy. The good news is that God built revival [into the redemption story]. The church ought to expect a revival; they ought to accept the fact that "if my people that are called by my name will humble themselves and pray and seek my face and turn from their wicked ways, God said that I will hear from heaven and forgive your sin" [2 Chronicles 7:14]. Isn't that good news?

I have been given so much opportunity. But [I ask myself], do we have the true divine conviction? Can we find a way to preach the truth in love? That's what I want to do with these last days.

Wright: At a previous conference, one of the presenters said, "The young college students I work with see Christianity as one of the greatest roadblocks to justice and to the common good. They don't see it as a force for good." Do you experience that among the people you work with? And what answer would you give?

Perkins: Yeah, exactly. If you've got to measure it, test it, that test would come out right. The church, religion, has been a roadblock. But what I'm saying is that truth goes marching on. Truth is the centrality of the gospel. The truth is the incarnation of God in Jesus Christ. This centrality—when Paul said, "I'm not ashamed of the gospel of Christ, for it is the power of God unto salvation" [Romans 1:16], he was talking about more than human effort.

Wright: We've had a wonderful time with you. Before we open the floor for questions, talk to us about this new book, *He Calls Me Friend: The Healing Power of Friendship in a Lonely World*. What's the genesis of this book?

Perkins: I think one of the most pressing questions in the Bible is, "Who is my neighbor?" [Luke 10:29]. But another one that is very powerful is in the book of Romans: Paul was trying to summarize the different needs of the Jews and the Gentiles. And he asks the question, "What did Abraham, our founding father, find when he found the most high God?" [Romans 4:1]. I think that's a question of questions in the Bible.

Moody Press came and said, "You've written all these books about 'how to.'" But they thought I hadn't ever done anything that gave the depths of my theological thought. They wanted a book about two hundred pages so somebody could put it in a briefcase and read it on a train to New York. [They said,] "We want you to state the essence of the gospel."

We got to thinking, what is the shortest version of why Jesus came? First John 1:7 says, "The blood of Jesus Christ, God's Son, cleanses us from all sin."

So, I then found that "he made us friends" was what kept us together. "And the word was made flesh, and dwelt among us." How do you maintain that unity? It's one thing to get unity, friendship, but to maintain a friendship? He said, "We walk in the light, as he's in the light. We have friendship one with another, and the blood of Jesus Christ, God's Son, cleanses us."

So this book is a follow-up to my manifesto. I meant for this book, *He Calls Me Friend*, to be my memoir, a reflection on my life.

Audience question: Can you share a little bit about your prayer life?

Perkins: It's better than it has ever been in my life. Trying to finish life now has become stressful. And I think that connects to aging— seeing suffering as a virtue. I also think that my prayer life is coming out of my pain in view of the blindness of our society.

In this book, there's a chapter on tolerance. People say, "I don't like tolerance. I don't want to just tolerate people. I want to love them." I understand what they're doing. But there's space for tolerance. Tolerance is set in space and time. It is for when you see somebody out there; they might look like an animal when you're far off. But when you get close enough that you can know them, they become human beings.

So tolerant is a good *time* element. To help us to know—don't kill it. Don't kill me too quick. And that's what I see in terms of policemen and young blacks. Don't kill me too quick. Don't kill me too quick.

Audience question: I was wondering how you keep your vitality and in your relationship with God and how that is manifested through prayer and your prayer life.

Perkins: Henri Nouwen helped me a lot. I like the little *Mornings with Henri.* We became friends, and I think I suffer from the same things he suffered—an extreme ego. So I think that the mind is conscious of trying to shine a light in this dark place that we're in right now. And I think that keeps me at least broken. I wake up broken. I wake up with the insanity. We're almost at the end of this hatred and genocide. Hating our own people. Black folks are killing black folks that are their cousins. This is the message—with a pistol it don't take long. White folks are killing each other, going into school with automatic weapons. That's what's burning me, these insane questions we ask. And then we make those questions bigger than grace. We make the question bigger than grace—grace is bigger than our sin.

O Lord, what a friend we have in Jesus. All our sin and griefs from sin he bears. What a privilege it is to carry everything to God in prayer. And to each other. We're connected.

Contributors

Katelyn Beaty is an acquisitions editor with Brazos Press. She began her career with *Christianity Today* as a copy editor, launched the women's website (Her.meneutics), and eventually became the magazine's youngest and first female managing editor. In 2016 she published her first book, *A Woman's Place: A Christian Vision for Your Calling in the Office, the Home, and the World*. She contributes to the *Washington Post*, the *Atlantic*, and the *New York Times*, and comments on faith and culture for CNN, ABC, NPR, the Associated Press, Religion News Service, the Canadian Broadcasting Corporation, and McClatchy Newspapers.

Christopher J. Devers is assistant professor of education at Johns Hopkins University and senior fellow for operations of the Lumen Research Institute. Overall, Devers is interested in applied metacognitive processes and how people learn. Specifically, he explores learning using videos and mobile devices, and in online environments. He is also interested in the scholarship of teaching and learning and student success.

Heather Templeton Dill is president of the John Templeton Foundation. Most recently, she served as executive liaison to the president. Prior to joining the foundation staff, she taught high school–level history, government, and economics in Pennsylvania. While living in Charlottesville, Virginia, she was a homeschool educator as well as a manuscript editor and research assistant at the University of Virginia. Dill is also currently a member of the board of First Trust Bank and previously served on the Templeton Religion Trust steering committee and the Templeton World Charity Foundation board.

Emmanuel Katongole is professor of theology and peace studies at the University of Notre Dame. A Catholic priest, he previously served as associate professor of theology and world Christianity at Duke University, where he was the codirector of the Center for Reconciliation. Katongole is the author of books on the Christian social imagination, the crisis of faith following the genocide in Rwanda, and Christian approaches to justice, peace, and reconciliation. His most recent book is *The Sacrifice of Africa: A Political Theology for Africa*.

Linda A. Livingstone is the president of Baylor University. She previously served as dean and professor of management at the George Washington University School of Business, from 2014 to 2017, and as dean of Pepperdine University's Graziadio School of Business and Management, from 2002 to 2014. As a scholar of organizational behavior, she has contributed to journals such as the *American Business Review*, the *Journal of Organizational Behavior*, and the *Journal of High Technology Management Research*, and to books such as *Business and Corporate Integrity: Sustaining Organizational Compliance, Ethics and Trust*.

George M. Marsden is professor of history emeritus at the University of Notre Dame. As one of the most distinguished historians of American Christianity, Marsden writes on topics such as evangelicalism and higher education. His most significant books include *Fundamentalism and American Culture*, *The Soul of the American University*, *The Outrageous Idea of Christian Scholarship*, and *The Twilight of the American Enlightenment*. His *Jonathan Edwards: A Life* won the Bancroft Prize in 2004.

Jerry Pattengale is university professor at Indiana Wesleyan University and codirector of the Lumen Research Institute. Previously, he also served as executive director of education at the Museum of the Bible (Washington, DC) and was one of its two founding scholars. Pattengale has authored over twenty books and contributes to a wide variety of outlets, including the *Wall Street Journal*, *Christianity Today*, the *Washington Post*, *Inside Higher Ed*, *Patheos*, the *Chicago Tribune*, and the History Channel.

John M. Perkins is a minister, civil rights leader, and community developer. He is the cofounder of the Christian Community Development Association and with his wife, Vera Mae Perkins, established the John and Vera Mae Perkins Foundation. The John M. Perkins Leadership Fellows Program at Calvin College and the John Perkins Center for Reconciliation, Leadership Training, and Community Development at Seattle Pacific University are both named in his honor and respectively seek to carry on the work to which Perkins has committed his life. He is also the author of numerous books, including *A Quiet Revolution*, *Welcoming Justice*, and *Dream with Me*.

Todd C. Ream is professor of higher education at Taylor University, senior fellow for programming with the Lumen Research Institute, and publisher for *Christian Scholar's Review*. Previously, Ream served on college and university campuses in residence life, student support services, and honors programs, and as a chief student development officer. He is the author and editor of many books and contributes to a wide variety of publications, including *About Campus*, *Christianity Today*, *First Things*, *Inside Higher Ed*, *Modern Theology*, *New Blackfriars*, *Notre Dame Magazine*, *The Review of Higher Education*, and *Teachers College Record*. He is presently working on a series of books concerning Theodore M. Hesburgh, CSC.

Miroslav Volf is the director of the Yale Center for Faith and Culture and the Henry B. Wright Professor of Theology at Yale University. He has written or edited more than twenty books and over ninety scholarly articles. His most significant books include *Exclusion and Embrace* (the recipient of the 2002 Grawemeyer Award), *After Our Likeness, Allah,* and *A Public Faith.* Volf has given many lectures, including the Dudleian Lecture at Harvard University, the Chavasse Lectures at the University of Oxford, the Waldenstroem Lectures at Stockholm University, the Gray Lectures at Duke University, and the Stob Lectures at Calvin College. He has also been featured on National Public Radio's *Speaking of Faith* and Public Television's *Religion and Ethics Newsweekly.*

David W. Wright is the president of Indiana Wesleyan University. Previously, he served as Indiana Wesleyan's provost and helped develop Wesley Seminary, the School of Nursing, the School of Health Sciences, the Ron Blue Institute for Financial Planning, and the National Conversations. Earlier in his career at Indiana Wesleyan, Wright led the university's entry into online education and initiated the regional campus development strategy. Beyond his tenure at Indiana Wesleyan University, Wright served as dean of the School of Theology at Azusa Pacific University and with theological education ministries for the Wesleyan Church in England and Haiti.

Amos Yong is dean of the School of Theology and the School of Intercultural Studies and professor of theology and mission at Fuller Theological Seminary. He has authored or edited almost four dozen volumes, including *The Future of Evangelical Theology, Renewing Christian Theology* (with Jonathan A. Anderson), *Interdisciplinary and Religio-cultural Discourses on a Spirit-Filled World* (coedited with Veli-Matti Kärkkäinen and Kirsteen Kim), *Pneumatology and the Christian-Buddhist Dialogue, The Cosmic Breath,* and *Spirit of Love.* Yong has also authored over two hundred articles for a wide range of peer-reviewed journals, edited collections, and other venues. He is the past president of the Society for Pentecostal Studies.

Index

Index

Index

Walls, Andrew, 113
Washington, George, 47
Washington Post, 83, 90, 139, 141
Washington University, 75
Wells, Sam, 109, 124-25
West, Cornel, 58
West Virginia University, 53
Wikipedia, 85
William & Mary, 47
Willow Creek Community Church, 92-94
Wilson-Hartgrove, Jonathan, xxxi, 113

Wirzba, Norman, 121
Wolterstorff, Nicholas, 15, 16
Word Made Flesh, 114
World Interfaith Harmony Week, 66
World Vision International, 114
Wright, N. T., 68
xenophobia, xxii
Yale University, xviii, xxvi, 5, 18, 46, 47, 141
Zacchaeus, 90
Zimmerman, Dean, 73-74